THE THEORY OF ECONOMIC POLICY
IN ENGLISH CLASSICAL POLITICAL ECONOMY

Also by Lord Robbins

AN ESSAY ON THE NATURE AND SIGNIFICANCE OF
    ECONOMIC SCIENCE

AUTOBIOGRAPHY OF AN ECONOMIST

THE EVOLUTION OF MODERN ECONOMIC THEORY

MONEY, TRADE AND INTERNATIONAL RELATIONS

POLITICAL ECONOMY: PAST AND PRESENT

POLITICS AND ECONOMICS

THE THEORY OF ECONOMIC DEVELOPMENT IN THE HISTORY
    OF ECONOMIC THOUGHT

THE THEORY
OF ECONOMIC POLICY

IN ENGLISH CLASSICAL
POLITICAL ECONOMY

BY

LORD ROBBINS

SECOND EDITION

PORCUPINE PRESS
Philadelphia

*First edition 1952
Reprinted 1953, 1961, 1965, 1970
Second edition 1978*

Published in the United Kingdom by
THE MACMILLAN PRESS LTD
London and Basingstoke

Published in the United States of America by
PORCUPINE PRESS
Philadelphia, Pennsylvania

Printed in Great Britain

Library of Congress Cataloging in Publication Data

Robbins, Lionel Charles, Robbins, Baron, 1898-
 The theory of economic policy in English
classical political economy.

 Bibliography: p.
 Includes index.
 1. Economic policy—History. 2. Economics—
Great Britain—History. I. Title.
[HD82.R64 1978]   338.941   78-2931
ISBN 0-87991-868-3

TO CAROLINE

THIS EXCURSION INTO A COMMON
BORDERLAND

CONTENTS

" Mr. Ricardo, with a very composed manner, has a continual life of mind, and starts perpetually new game in conversation. I never argued or discussed a question with any person who argues more fairly or less for victory and more for truth. He gives full weight to every argument brought against him, and seems not to be on any side of the question for one instant longer than the conviction of his mind on that side. It seems quite indifferent to him whether you find the truth, or whether he finds it, provided it be found. One gets at something by conversing with him ; one learns either that one is wrong or that one is right, and the understanding is improved without the temper being ever tried in the discussion." (Maria Edgeworth, in a letter to Mrs. Edgeworth, November 9, 1821, printed in *A Memoir of Maria Edgeworth with a Selection from her Letters*, by the late Mrs. Edgeworth, edited by her children, Vol. II, page 151.)

PREFACE TO THE SECOND EDITION

THE demand for a second edition of these lectures comes at what, for their author, is a congenial moment. At the conclusion of the last lecture in this book, having repudiated, in that context, appraisal of the theories which it recorded, I expressed an interest in such an enterprise; and quite recently, after an interval of many years, in my *Political Economy: Past and Present*, I made an attempt of just that kind. The two works therefore have some sort of organic connection. *The Theory of Economic Policy in English Classical Political Economy* is a straightforward account of what I believe to be the main propositions of an historical position : *Political Economy: Past and Present* is, among other things, a normative reconsideration of that position in the light of subsequent economic developments and necessary analytical modifications.

In re-reading a work whose origins, as related in the Preface to the First Edition, go back to lectures at the London School of Economics delivered before the Second World War, I am a little surprised to find that I have so little to recant. Needless to say the views here presented have not escaped criticism : so many people have committed themselves to a contrary view of the Classical Economists, both their conceptions of appropriate policy and their alleged interested motives, that it must be annoying to them to find their position called in question. But this has left me unruffled ; and, although I know nowadays many more references which might have driven home my interpretations, I am still convinced that my broad perspective is historically valid.

The one implicit criticism which I would, naturally, take seriously is Professor Hutchinson's query concerning the validity of including Jeremy Bentham as a Classical Economist. This, I should agree, is a matter on which reasonable people may take two views. I thoroughly concur in the judgement that certainly in some matters of finance Bentham must be judged — as indeed he was by Ricardo — as standing apart from the main tradition. But I did not deal at any length with monetary policy in this book except to point out that while the Classical School, defined as I have defined it, certainly regarded the issue of the means of exchange as involving state regulation, on the question of what that regulation should be they were certainly at sixes and sevens.[1] But I would submit that, as regards the general theory of economic policy, Bentham's *Manual of Political Economy* — composite though we now know that to be — and his close connection with James Mill, Ricardo and even with John Stuart Mill provide some warrant for the citation of his views in the context of these lectures.

There is one section in these lectures which has escaped critical strictures, apart from a friendly suggestion of some exaggeration from Lord Roll in the last edition of his distinguished *History of Economic Thought*, (fn. p. 144) namely the contrast in the second lecture between the philosophical foundations of the Physiocratic and the English Classical approach to the functions of the state in general. Here I hold firmly to my main position. There seems to me to be a world of difference between the

---

[1] I have dealt with some aspects of this complex problem in sundry other works : my *Robert Torrens and the Evolution of Classical Economics* (1958) ; *The Theory of Economic Development in the History of Economic Thought* (1968) ; The *Introduction* to the Toronto Edition of J. S. Mill's *Essays on Economics and Society* (1967) reprinted in my *Evolution of Modern Economic Theory* (1970) and in *Political Economy Past and Present* (1976) — all (except the Toronto Edition) published by Macmillan, London.

naturrechtlich outlook of Quesnay and his followers and the broad utilitarianism of David Hume and the more ambiguous, though in effect utilitarian, system of Adam Smith.[1] In the original lecture I did concede to Gonnard " that the empirical and utilitarian point of view is far from being absent " from the Physiocrats. I now think, however, that my treatment of this interesting subject might have been rather more extensive than the existing text.

There is one respect in which, if I were writing these lectures today, the draft would have been decidedly different. In my introductory remarks to the first lecture at Manchester, my tone was almost apologetic. I defended the History of Economic Thought as a subject and congratulated my hosts for providing for its study. That attitude would clearly be inappropriate today. There are indeed some institutions, both here and in the United States, where the virtual total neglect of anything of the sort would suggest the attitude I was regretting ; and there is certainly room elsewhere for further improvement. But the spread of interest in the subject in the last few years, the notable contributions, for example, of Professors Collison Black, Hollander, Hutchinson, O'Brien, Robertson, Stigler, Winch and many others, the appearance of scholarly editions of historical works of which the Sraffa Edition of Ricardo, the Glasgow Edition of Adam Smith, the Toronto Edition of John Stuart Mill and the invaluable translation of Walras' *Elements* and the collection of his letters by Professor Jaffé are examples, the existence of special journals and special societies devoted to the subject,

---

[1] On Adam Smith's use of the principle of utility, Professor T. D. Campbell's *Adam Smith's Science of Morals* (1971) casts a most valuable light. See especially pp. 206–20.

would today render such diffidence regarding my choice of subject somewhat odd.

The main addition to the present edition is a footnote citation on page 168 of a passage from Mill's *Liberty* on nationalization which I think considerably reinforces the argument of the chapter in which I deal with Mill's ambiguities as regards socialism.

I owe to Mr Duncan Forbes a correction regarding the nature of both Hume and Smith's political outlook to which I have endeavoured to do justice in the relevant sentence on page 3 (see his most illuminating paper on " Sceptical Whiggism, Commerce and Liberty " in *Essays on Adam Smith*, edited by Andrew S. Skinner and Thomas Wilson, Oxford, 1976).

ROBBINS

THE LONDON SCHOOL OF ECONOMICS
September 1977

PREFACE TO THE FIRST EDITION

THE following pages owe their origin to a short course of lectures on *Theories of Economic Policy* which I delivered at the London School of Economics in 1939. The main views which they contain were all set forth in the two lectures there devoted to the Classical system. But the limitations of time within which I had to work left me dissatisfied with my treatment and I contemplated a further development before publication.

Then came the war with nearly six years' suspension of academic activities, and after that three more very strenuous years in which the reconstruction of our faculty arrangements absorbed most of the waking hours of my life. So that it was not until last year, when the University of Manchester did me the honour of asking me to deliver the Simon Lectures for 1950, that I was able once more to take up my investigations where I had left them in 1939. The work this involved was embodied in the first three lectures of the present book, which, although somewhat expanded, remain in substance as they were then delivered. I owe my many friends at Manchester a deep debt of gratitude, not only for their invitation and their kindly tolerance as listeners, but also for sending me back to a branch of our subject which I have always found especially congenial.

When, however, I came to revise these three lectures for publication, it seemed to me that, even on the very broad plane of generalization which I had chosen, my treatment would be lacking if I did not add sections dealing with the attitude of the Classical Economists to

socialism and with their more general position in the
history of social philosophy. An invitation in the spring
of this year to hold a visiting fellowship at the Institute
for Advanced Study at Princeton, supplemented by a
generous travelling grant from the Rockefeller Foundation, afforded an ideal opportunity in which to carry
through the necessary work, which in the end proved to
involve a doubling of the original number of lectures.
I should like to express my warmest thanks to Dr.
Robert Oppenheimer, the Director of the Institute, and
to Dr. Walter Stewart, the head of the Economics
Section, for the unforgettable kindness and hospitality
which I enjoyed as their guest.

The introductory section of Lecture I sets forth the
scope and the limitations of my intentions and these
are again emphasized in the concluding section of
Lecture VI. There is, therefore, no need for me to
repeat myself on that score in this preface. I ought,
however, perhaps to add one further word regarding
my method of presentation. The argument of the
lectures involves a view of the Classical system which,
although I am sure it would have seemed obvious to
an earlier generation, must appear as novel and perhaps
paradoxical to many contemporary readers. I have,
therefore, had recourse to copious quotations from
the original texts, preferring that the authors I discuss
should speak in their own words rather than that I
should run the risk of misrepresenting them by oblique
reference. I have done this with all the better con-
science, in that most of them had a command of phrase
and exposition greatly superior to anything I could
hope to achieve by paraphrase. In quoting at length,
therefore, I conceive that I accomplish two purposes :
I provide demonstration, more convincing than otherwise would be possible, of the interpretations which I

put forward ; and, at the same time, I present to a generation of readers, largely unacquainted with their excellence, specimens of exposition and argument which, whatever the deficiencies of my accompanying comments, should provide some net compensation for the trouble of reading the book.

In thus presenting these lectures to the public, I hope I shall not be thought to be making any high claims to originality or new contributions to scholarship. My subject is not one on which, at this time of day, it would be easy to be very original without risking distortion of important facts ; moreover, my indebtedness to others is abundantly evident in my references. As for scholarship, it has been my good fortune to know some of the really great scholars in this field ; and I hope that I know my place. All that I would claim as a justification for publication is that the assembling of the material in this form may perhaps be useful to students and may also — although I am not very hopeful in this respect — be some safeguard for a few years against the grosser forms of misunderstanding and misrepresentation of which, in recent years, this aspect of the Classical system has all too frequently been the subject.

Many friends have helped me with criticism and advice. I will not name them lest they should be involved in any disapprobation I may incur ; they know, I hope, that I am sincerely grateful. I must, however, explicitly tender thanks for invaluable editorial labours to Miss Helen Beven, secretary to the economics department at the School of Economics, and to my daughter, Anne Robbins.

LIONEL ROBBINS

The London School of Economics
April 1951

THE SYSTEM OF ECONOMIC FREEDOM

If I had been speaking before almost any other audience I should have felt obliged to preface my remarks by some apology for my subject. When I began to study economics, thirty years ago, the senior generation of economists in this country — Marshall, Edgeworth, Foxwell and Cannan — were all men who, in their different ways, were truly learned in what may be called the scholarship of the subject; and some acquaintance with the history of economic thought was usually deemed to be a desirable part of the equipment of the economist. But, in the years that have passed since then, all that has changed. In most centres of study, this kind of knowledge has come to be regarded as a very unimportant embellishment, as inessential to the economist as a knowledge of the history of chemistry is said to be inessential to the chemist. This development has always seemed to me to be unfortunate. I do not think that, even in the purely analytical field, our knowledge is so far advanced as to justify us in writing off as superseded the propositions of all but our immediate contemporaries; and, in the applied field, I do not think that we can hope to understand the problems and policies of our own day if we do not know the problems and policies out of which they grew. I suspect that damage has been done, not merely to historical and speculative culture, but also to our practical insight, by this indifference to our intellectual past — this provincialism in time — which has become so characteristic of our particular branch of social studies. When, therefore, the other day your University, which has so often led the way in important developments in our subject, decided to create a special post for the study of the history of economic thought, in my judgment it set a notable example, which I hope will be widely followed. Certainly it made a gesture which must greatly relieve the diffidence of any guest who comes, as I do, with a desire to make a modest contribution in this particular field.

(i) *Subject and Plan of the Lectures*

May I begin by delimiting my subject ? I wish to present a brief survey of the theory of economic policy of the English Classical Economists. By the theory of economic policy I mean the general body of principles of governmental action or inaction — the *agenda* or *non-agenda* of the state as Bentham [1] called them — in regard to economic activity. By the English Classical Economists I mean the two great Scotch philosophers, David Hume and Adam Smith, and their followers, most of whom belonged to the first two generations of the London Political Economy Club — conspicuously, Ricardo, Malthus, Torrens, Senior, McCulloch and the two Mills. I include also Jeremy Bentham, who was much more important as an economist than is often recognized ; and I shall not refrain from quoting Cairnes, who came later, but who, in some important respects, is to be regarded as one of the main expositors of the Classical position. You will observe that in my title I deliberately

---

[1] Bentham, *Manual of Political Economy*: *Works* (edited Bowring), vol. iii, pp. 35, 41 *seq.*

exclude any economists other than inhabitants of this island.[1] I should like also, even at this stage, to make clear, what I hope will become very apparent later on, that I do not regard the Classical School and the so-called Manchester School as identical — very much the contrary indeed.

Now, of course, it would be a great mistake to regard the men I have named as being in every respect a homogeneous group. The picture which has been drawn of the Political Economy Club as the assembly of a new church imbued with " all the spirit of ecclesiastical fervour "[2] was always hard to reconcile with the known facts of the disputes between Ricardo and Malthus and between Tooke and Overstone; and the publication of the diaries of J. L. Mallet[3] have deprived it of the last vestige of plausibility. Nevertheless, on the broader issues, they undoubtedly held certain principles in common : they would have subscribed to the central thesis of the *Wealth of Nations* against Mercantilism ; they believed in property and free enterprise ; the main drift of the *Essay on Population* was accepted by most of them. They varied in politics. Hume and Smith were " sceptical Whigs "; Senior and Malthus were less uncommitted that way ; Bentham, Ricardo and the two

---

[1] This for two reasons. First, for reasons of space : these lectures would become a treatise if I were to take account of all the continental writers who have been called classical by someone or other. Secondly, for reasons of interpretation : I have no desire to be insular in outlook, but I am clear that the theories I am about to examine originated predominantly in this country, that beyond a vague derivation from the *Wealth of Nations*, the continental writers have little or no organic relation with the movement over here, and that indeed it is the differences, in this connexion, between English and continental theories rather than the similarities, which are significant for the history of thought.

[2] Sir W. Ashley, " Address to the British Association ", Economic Section, Leicester, 1907, reprinted in the *Economic Journal*, vol. xvii, p. 467 *seq.*

[3] *Political Economy Club, Minutes of Proceedings, etc.*, 1821–1920, especially p. 217. " I do not apprehend," says Mallet, " if we were in the habit of voting *aye* or *no* on the questions proposed, that there would have been half a dozen occasions since the establishment of the club, 6 years ago, in which anything like unanimity would have prevailed."

Mills, Philosophical Radicals.   But they shared a common interest in economic reform, which manifested itself, not so much in common support of specific measures — though there was much of that — as in a commonly held belief that the application of certain methods of approach and analysis, the recently discovered science of Political Economy, offered superior hopes for what they would have called improvement.   They would have repudiated a wooden adherence to minutely fixed doctrines.   But they would have acknowledged the use of a more or less common language and a common interest in social betterment.

For good or for bad, these men and their ideas are historically important.   They exercised a profound influence on public opinion in this country.   They were responsible, directly or indirectly, for many far-reaching legislative and administrative changes.   Even to-day, in innumerable ways of which we are seldom aware, their outlook continues to affect ours.   Nor is this influence confined to this country.   It is true that the specifically Ricardian element in Classical analysis did not prove a hardy migrant and was rarely understood abroad.   But the broader theory of policy, based on Smith and Hume and Bentham, although often misconceived, has certainly been very influential.   It is no exaggeration to say that it is impossible to understand the evolution and the meaning of Western liberal civilization without some understanding of Classical Political Economy.

But, for all this, it is very little understood.   It is true that as a result of the labours of a few outstanding scholars — chiefly outside this country, I am sorry to say — many parts of this subject have been better surveyed and analysed than ever before.   But the main body of contemporary opinion shows little awareness of this ; and understanding of the system which once dominated the social thought of the West is becoming confined to a handful of specialists. Indeed, the position is much worse than this. Popular writing in this connexion is far below the zero of knowledge or common decency. On this plane, not only is any real knowledge of the Classical writers non-existent but, further, their place has been taken by a set of mythological figures, passing by the same names, but not infrequently invested with attitudes almost the exact reverse of those which the originals adopted. These dummies are very malignant creatures indeed. They are the tools or lacqueys of capitalist exploiters — I think that has the authentic stylistic flavour. They are indefatigable opponents of social reform. They can conceive no function for the state other than that of the night watchman. They "defend" subsistence wages and are supremely indifferent to the well-being of the working classes. Hence, when a popular writer of the day wishes to present his own point of view in a specially favourable setting, he has only to point the contrast with the attitude of these reprehensible people and the desired effect is produced. You would be surprised at the number of well-known authors who have resorted to this device.

Now, doubtless, the best remedy for this state of affairs would be that people should once more turn to the original texts. I hope that this, in fact, is what will happen in those universities which are once more insisting on some minimum knowledge of the history of economic thought. But, since life is short and the literature is extensive, there is perhaps something to be said for yet another attempt to get the wide field into something like a correct focus. That, at any rate, is what I want to do in these lectures.

The plan which I propose is as follows : in this first lecture I shall try to set out certain broad aspects of

the Classical conception of the ends of economic activity
and the general system of organization best adapted
to meet these ends ; in the second lecture I shall discuss the Classical theory of the economic functions of
the state ; in the third I shall discuss the attitude of
the Classical Economists to the so-called problem of the
condition of the people ; in the fourth and fifth I shall
try to bring together the various bits and pieces of what
they said about collectivism, with some special attention
in the fifth to the attitude of John Stuart Mill ; in the
sixth I shall stand back and try to see the movement as
a whole in a setting of the history of social philosophy.

I should like to end these introductory remarks by
making quite plain the limitations of my intentions.
Throughout the entire plan that I have outlined to you
my aim is to describe and to analyse rather than to judge.
I want to explain to you the facts of a certain phase in
the history of thought ; I do not want, in this place, to
make any appraisal of these facts in the sense of an
inquiry into the ultimate validity of the doctrines
involved.   Therefore when I set out as clearly as I can
the theories which the Classical Economists held on
particular issues of policy and their reasons for holding
such views, or when I distinguish the theories which they
held from the theories which they have been alleged to
hold, you must not interpret me as presenting you with
my own point of view on these matters.   I will not
conceal from you that I have a considerable admiration
for some of these men, both as human beings and as
writers, and that I believe that many of the aims for
which they stood are still important to humanity.   But
to disentangle what I believe to be right in their formulations from what I believe to be wrong would be a task
far transcending the possible limits of these lectures, and
I have therefore very deliberately not attempted it.

All that I intend is to try to help you to understand
what the Classical Economists were trying to do and
to provide some sort of guide to what they actually said.

(ii) *The Object of Economic Activity*

If you had asked any Classical Economist to what final
end economic activity was supposed to be directed, or
by what ultimate criterion its success was to be estimated,
I do not think the issue would have been in doubt.

" Consumption ", said Adam Smith, " is the sole end
and purpose of all production ; and the interest of the
producer ought to be attended to, only so far as it is
necessary for promoting that of the consumer." [1]

James Mill was no less emphatic. " Of the four sets
of operations, Production, Distribution, Exchange and
Consumption, which constitute the subject of Political
Economy," he says, " the first three are means. No
man produces for the sake of producing and nothing
further. Distribution, in the same manner, is not performed for the sake of distribution. Things are distributed as also exchanged, to some end.

" That end is consumption." [2]

Nothing could seem clearer than that. But as
usual in our peculiar subject, which is always trying to
trap the complexities of will and deed in the simplicity
of language, qualifications and elucidations are needed.

First, about the producers. Adam Smith and his
followers were unequivocally opposed to any fostering
of producer interest as such ; for that, they thought,
involved sectional privilege and therefore damage to the
community as a whole. But this view was forward-
looking ; it forbade the creation of new producer

---

[1] *Wealth of Nations* (Cannan's edition), vol. ii, p. 159.
[2] *Elements of Political Economy* (3rd edition), p. 219.

privilege. As regards existing privileges, while it was one of their main objectives eventually to do away with them, it would be a mistake to suppose that they always favoured immediate and drastic extinction. Some regard to existing expectations, some mitigation of the effects of change, seemed to be dictated by general considerations of utility ; it will be found that even Ricardo recommended reduction of the Corn Duties by stages [1] and was quite explicit why he did so.

Furthermore, although the interests of producers as such were never to be taken as the criterion, there was no suggestion that producers were to be forced against their will into occupations which they found less attractive, taking everything into account, than others. The satisfactions associated with particular types of production, the pleasures of workmanship, the enjoyment of certain ways of life, were to be counted, as it were, as pleasures of consumption ; and if a man preferred them to the increased consumption of other things which he could obtain by working elsewhere, there was no presumption whatever that this was in any way undesirable. I do not know any cut-and-dried statement to this effect by the Classical writers. But it is the clear implication of the doctrine of the tendency in a state of economic freedom, to equality, not of money wages but of net advantages ; and this, of course, was common to all of them. [2]

Secondly, by consumption is to be understood not only consumption now but also consumption in the future. It has sometimes been made a reproach to the Classical Economists that, in making consumption the end of economic activity, they ignored the desirability of creat-

---

[1] *Works* (edited McCulloch) : *On Protection to Agriculture*, p. 493.

[2] The *locus classicus* is the chapter in the *Wealth of Nations* on Wages and Profit (Cannan's edition), vol. i, p. 101 *seq*.

ing productive power. List is the great assailant here ; his diatribe against Adam Smith in his *National System of Political Economy* is based precisely on this accusation.[1] Now it may well be that the Classical Economists paid less attention to the forcing of manufacturing industry than List and his followers thought desirable ; there will be more to be said about this later. But, in the light of the stress which the majority of them laid on the importance of accumulation, the suggestion that they did not consider the importance of increasing productive power seems to rest on crude misunderstanding. The distinction between productive and unproductive consumption was devised to reinforce just this emphasis.[2]

Thirdly, we should note that by consumption is meant not only the consumption of private individuals, the benefit of which is limited to themselves, but also the consumption of government services such as defence, the benefit of which is indiscriminate. There will be much more to be said about these services later on when we are discussing the functions of the state. But at this early stage it is necessary to observe that, from Adam Smith onwards, it was recognized that such services might be " in the highest degree advantageous to a great society ".[3] It is quite wrong to suppose that they were ignored.

Finally, it must be realized that this consumption which was regarded as the end of economic activity was the consumption of a limited community, the members of the nation-state. To the extent to which they repudiated former maxims of economic warfare and

---

[1] *The National System of Political Economy*, by Friedrich List (translated by Samson S. Lloyd, 1904), chapter xii, p. 108 *seq.*
[2] See Adam Smith, *op. cit.* vol. i, pp. 320-331; also N. W. Senior. *An Outline of the Science of Political Economy*, p. 54.
[3] Adam Smith, *op. cit.* vol. ii, p. 214.

assumed mutual advantage in international exchange, it is true that the outlook of the Classical Economists seems, and indeed is, more spacious and pacific than that of their antagonists.[1] But there is little evidence that they often went beyond the test of national advantage as a criterion of policy,[2] still less that they were prepared to contemplate the dissolution of national bonds. If you examine the ground on which they recommended free trade, you will find that it is always in terms of a more productive use of *national* resources : I do not think that Adam Smith's dictum that " defence . . . is of much more importance than opulence " [3] was called in question by any of them.[4] I find no trace anywhere in their writings of the vague cosmopolitanism with which they are often credited by continental writers.[5] I do not claim this as a virtue — or as a deficiency ; the question of the extent to which, at that stage of history, it was incumbent on political thinkers to transcend the ideas and the criteria of the nation-state is a matter of great difficulty. All that I contend is that we get our picture wrong if we suppose that the English Classical

[1] See, *e.g.*, Hume's declaration in his essay, " Of the Jealousy of Trade ", that " not only as a man, but as a BRITISH subject, I pray for the flourishing commerce of *Germany, Spain, Italy*, and even *France* itself ", *Essays, Moral, Political and Literary* (edited Green and Grose), vol. i, p. 348.

[2] In Bentham's *Manual of Political Economy* : *op. cit.* vol. iii, p. 35, there is a parenthetic reference to the " *mundane* " stock of wealth. But this is very exceptional.

[3] Adam Smith, *op. cit.* vol. i, p. 429.

[4] It is interesting to note that Mill favoured conscription. *Letters of John Stuart Mill* (edited Elliot), vol. ii, p. 291.

[5] *E.g.* List, *op. cit.* chapter xi. Adam Smith (*Theory of Moral Sentiments*, part vi, section ii) expressly repudiates it : " France may contain, perhaps, near three times the number of inhabitants which Great Britain contains. In the great society of mankind, therefore, the prosperity of France should appear to be of much greater importance than that of Great Britain. The British subject, however, who upon that account, should prefer upon all occasions the prosperity of the former to that of the latter country would not be thought a good citizen of Great Britain. We do not love our country merely as part of the great society of mankind : we love it for its own sake and independently of any such consideration."

Economists would have recommended, because it was good for the world at large, a measure which they thought would be harmful to their own community. It was the consumption of the national economy which they regarded as the end of economic activity.

(iii) *The System of Economic Freedom*

It is the specific contribution of the Classical Economists, that for the achievement of this end they recommended what Marshall called the System of Economic Freedom. Given a certain framework of law and order and certain necessary governmental services (of which much more hereafter), they conceived that the object of economic activity was best attained by a system of spontaneous co-operation. As consumers, the citizens should be free to buy what best pleased their fancy. As producers, as workers or as owners and organizers of the means of production, they should be free to use their labour power or their property in ways which, in their judgment, would bring them the maximum reward in money or satisfaction. It is the impersonal mechanism of the market which, on this view, brings it about that the interests of the different individuals are harmonized. To use Adam Smith's famous phrase, the individual seeking to direct industry that its produce may be of the greatest value "intends only his own gain", but "he is in this, as in many other cases, led by an invisible hand to promote an end which was no part of his intention ".[1] It follows that it should be a prime object of policy that trade and industry should be free, and that where obstacles to this spontaneous co-operation exist, they should be swept away. " The request which agriculture, manufactures,

[1] Adam Smith, *Wealth of Nations* (Cannan's edition) vol. i, p. 421.

and commerce present to governments ", said Bentham,
" is modest and reasonable as that which Diogenes made
to Alexander : ' Stand out of my sunshine '. We have no
need of favour — we require only a secure and open
path." [1]

Now, I shall be arguing in the next lecture that you
get an entirely distorted view of the significance of this
doctrine unless you see it in combination with the theory
of law and the functions of government which its authors
also propounded ; the idea of freedom *in vacuo* was
entirely alien to their conceptions. But there can be
no doubt that it was central in their system. It inspired
their crusade against what they considered to be abuses
of authority. It dictated their conception of what the
positive functions of the state should be. You cannot
understand their attitude to any important concrete
measure of policy unless you understand their belief with
regard to the nature and effects of the system of spontaneous co-operation. For this reason, before we can go any
further, it is necessary to devote some time to discovering
exactly what it was. This is perhaps the least interesting
part of our subject, since it is certainly more discussed
than the rest. But it is so often incorrectly put that,
although I am reluctant to run the risk of boring you,
I cannot afford to take for granted as known the
version which I believe to be correct. However, I shall
use a very broad brush and try to confine myself to
essentials.

As I see it, this belief in the System of Economic
Freedom rested on a twofold basis : belief in the desirability of freedom of choice for the consumer and belief
in the effectiveness, in meeting this choice, of freedom
on the part of producers. Each of these beliefs had a
positive and negative aspect : there were reasons why

[1] Bentham, *Manual of Political Economy* : *op. cit.* vol. iii, p. 35.

freedom was positively desirable, there were reasons why the alternative was inferior.

Let us begin with freedom for the consumer. Here matters are very simple. From the positive point of view, the adult consumer is held to be the best judge of his own interest. There are exceptions to this. There are abundant acknowledgments that the consumer must be protected in one way or another from fraud.[1] And, of course, it is not argued that the exercise of consumers' choice in the market is the best possible mechanism for bringing into being goods and services affording indiscriminate benefit. But, subject to these exceptions, the argument of Bentham is typical of the general attitude : "Generally speaking," says Bentham, "there is no one who knows what is for your interest so well, as yourself — no one who is disposed with so much ardour and constancy to pursue it."[2]

From the negative point of view, the argument is two-sided. Interference with this freedom involves coercion and therefore pain. Moreover, the choice that government makes for you is likely to be poor.[3] It must be remembered that the Classical Economists were opposing a conscious paternalism. The mercantile and cameralistic writers did not hesitate to propose all sorts of interferences with this kind of freedom. Bentham quotes "a large political work of M. Beausobre, counsellor to the King of Prussia", who, in the interests of population, recommends that "It is proper to watch during the fruit season lest the people eat that which is not ripe", and who, in the interests of the same good

---

[1] *E.g.* Ricardo, *Proposals for an Economical and Secure Currency* : *Works* (edited McCulloch), p. 408, follows Adam Smith in approving the government stamp on plate, and himself approves interference to ensure the purity of drugs and the competence of doctors.

[2] Bentham, *Manual of Political Economy* : *op. cit.* vol. iii, p. 33.

[3] *Ibid.* p. 33.

cause, urges that " men should be hindered from marrying very disagreeable women ".[1]

The argument for freedom of producers is, of course, more complicated. The positive argument is in two stages. In the first place, emphasis is laid upon the desirability of harnessing the machinery of production to the powerful and ubiquitous force of self-interest — not necessarily egotism : self-interest means the interest of oneself and the intimate circle to whom one spontaneously acknowledges obligation. No available force is as strong as this. " Man has almost constant occasion for the help of his brethren," says Adam Smith, " and it is in vain for him to expect it from their benevolence only. He will be more likely to prevail if he can interest their self-love in his favour, and show them that it is for their own advantage to do for him what he requires of them. Whoever offers to another a bargain of any kind, proposes to do this : Give me that which I want, and you shall have this which you want, is the meaning of every such offer ; and it is in this manner that we obtain from one another the far greater part of those good offices which we stand in need of. It is not from the benevolence of the butcher, the brewer, or the baker, that we expect our dinner, but from their regard to their own interest. We address ourselves not to their humanity but to their self-love." [2] Even J. S. Mill, who would have dearly liked to believe in the efficacy of other incentives, was quite clear that " in the imperfect degree of moral cultivation which mankind have yet reached " no general substitute was available. In his posthumously published *Chapters on Socialism*, which contain his final recorded thoughts on this subject, he says : " In the case of most men the only inducement which has been found suffi-

---

[1] Bentham, *op. cit.* vol. iii, p. 75, footnote.
[2] Adam Smith, *op. cit.* vol. i, p. 16.

ciently constant and unflagging to overcome the ever-present influence of indolence and love of ease, and induce men to apply themselves unrelaxingly to work for the most part in itself dull and unexciting, is the prospect of bettering their own economic condition and that of their family . . . to suppose the contrary would be to imply that with men as they now are, duty and honour are more powerful principles of action than personal interest, not solely as to special acts and for-bearances respecting which those sentiments have been exceptionally cultivated, but in the regulation of their whole lives ; which no one, I suppose, will affirm ".[1]

Now turn to the second stage of the argument. The *motive* for production, as we have just seen, is conceived to be self-interest. But the *guidance* of this motive so that it conduces to the interest of all concerned, is conceived to be brought about by the mechanism of the market and the force of competition. Given the conditions of demand, if the supplies available in any market can command a price which brings to the producers gains higher than they can get elsewhere and if markets are free, there is an incentive for more producers to move in, withdrawing their resources from other markets where the value of what they produce is less and augmenting the supply where the value of what they produce is more. Thus, according to Adam Smith, " the quantity of every commodity brought to the market naturally suits itself to the effectual demand. It is the interest of all those who employ their land, labour or stock in bringing any commodity to market that the quantity should never exceed the effectual demand : and it is the interest of all other people that it should never fall short of that demand." [2] The terminology

---

[1] *Fortnightly Review* (1879), vol. xxv (New Series), p. 516.
[2] Adam Smith, *op. cit.* vol. i, p. 59.

is not necessarily what we should use. But it is the essential opportunity cost doctrine.

And that, I believe, is about as far as we ought to go in reading modern refinements into this aspect of the classical case for economic freedom. Of course, in the theory of international trade, the analysis was carried much further : the overt statement of the theory of comparative advantage by Torrens, Ricardo and Senior [1] was a great advance on Adam Smith's very loose and often definitely erroneous propositions about this matter. But it is clear that the claims of the Classical Economists for competition and the market do not rest upon any very precise mathematical or semi-mathematical conceptions of statical equilibrium. Indeed, I cannot help suspecting that if they had been confronted with the systems of this sort which have been developed since their day, they would have had some hesitation in acknowledging a near family relationship. Their conception of the mechanism of the System of Economic Freedom was surely a conception of something more rough and ready, something much more dynamic and real than these exquisite laboratory models. Their claim, in essence, was not so much that the system of markets was always tending to some refined equilibrium adjustment, but rather that it provided a rough pointer and a rough discipline whereby the tumultuous forces of self-interest were guided and held in check. [2]

Thus Bentham argues that " Free competition is equivalent to a reward granted to those who furnish the

---

[1] Torrens, *An Essay on the External Corn Trade* (1815), pp. 264-266. Ricardo, *Principles* : *Works* (edited McCulloch), chapter vii, p. 72 *seq.* Senior, *Lectures on the Cost of Obtaining Money* : *Lecture I, passim.*

[2] On this point there is a very interesting discussion in Dr. Hla Myint's *Theories of Welfare Economics*, chapter iv. I should hesitate to accept in its entirety Dr. Myint's reinterpretation. But with what he says on the difference of tone between the Classical outlook and that of the neo-Classical writers, I am in considerable agreement.

best goods at the lowest price. It offers an immediate
and natural reward, which a crowd of rivals flatter themselves that they shall obtain, and acts with greater
efficacy than a distant punishment, from which each
may hope to escape." [1] And again in another place,
" By two opposite competitions prices are fixed. Competition among the purchasers secures to the producers
a sufficient compensation for the outlay of their capital
and labour : competition among the sellers, serving as
a counterpoise to the other, produces a cheap market and
reduces the prices of commodities to the lowest sum for
which it is worth while to produce them. The difference
between a low price and a high price is a reward offered
to the purchaser by one seller for the service he will
render to him, by granting what remains to be gained,
to him instead of to his competitor who requires more." [2]

This positive claim was, of course, strongly reinforced in their minds and in their arguments by the
negative belief that all alternative arrangements were
inferior. It is sometimes said that their reliance on enterprise and the market was due to the fact that they lived
at a day when the apparatus of administration was
manifestly inadequate to the general conduct of industry.
Up to a point, no doubt, that is true ; the bureaucracies
of their time were on the whole poorly staffed and inadequate even to much more essential functions. But
the implication that this was all that there was in their
attitude and that had they been privileged to envisage
a governmental machine as efficient, shall we say, as the
Civil Service in contemporary Britain, their scepticism
would have collapsed, seems to me to be unwarranted.
There is much more than that in Adam Smith's famous
dictum that " The statesman, who should attempt to

---

[1] Bentham, *Principles of Penal Law* : *op. cit.* vol. i, p. 534.
[2] *The Rationale of Reward* : *op. cit.* vol. ii, p. 228.

direct private people in what manner they ought to employ their capitals, would not only load himself with a most unnecessary attention, but assume an authority which could safely be trusted, not only to no single person, but to no council or senate whatever, and which would nowhere be so dangerous as in the hands of a man who had folly and presumption enough to fancy himself fit to exercise it ".[1] Or, remember his contemptuous description of Colbert: " A man of probity, of great industry, and knowledge of detail ; of great experience and acuteness in the examination of public accounts, and of abilities ; in short, every way fitted for introducing method and good order into the collection and expenditure of the public revenue. That minister had, unfortunately, embraced all the prejudices of the mercantile system, in its nature and essence a system of restraint and regulation, and such as could scarce fail to be agreeable to a laborious and plodding man of business, who had been accustomed to regulate the different public offices, and to establish the necessary checks and controls for confining each to its proper sphere. The industry and commerce of a great country he endeavoured to regulate upon the same model as the departments of a public office ; and instead of allowing every man to pursue his own interest his own way, upon the liberal plan of equality, liberty, and justice, he bestowed upon certain branches of industry extraordinary privileges, while he laid others under as extraordinary restraints." [2] I do not believe that the fundamental attitude underlying all this would have been likely to be dispelled by the realization of the possibility of less corruption and more efficiency in the working of the machinery of government. After all, Bentham devoted much attention to just this matter ; he may well be regarded as

---

[1] Adam Smith, *op. cit.* vol. i, p. 421.   [2] *Ibid.* vol. ii, p. 161.

the father of the modern civil service. Yet, as regards
the organization of the production of discriminate benefit,
he was no less individualist than Adam Smith. The
attitude of John Stuart Mill is much more ambiguous ;
but that is a matter with which I shall have to deal at
length later on.

But be all this as it may, there can be no doubt that
the English Classical Economists regarded their system
as something vastly superior in its implications for
human happiness than the systems of restraint and
regulation which then prevailed. We do not get these
men in their proper historical setting unless we realize
that, in the context of their day at least, they were
reformers. The System of Economic Freedom was not
just a detached recommendation not to interfere : it
was an urgent demand that what were thought to be
hampering and anti-social impediments should be removed and that the immense potential of free pioneering
individual initiative should be released. And, of course,
it was in this spirit that, in the world of practice, its
proponents addressed themselves to agitation against the
main forms of these impediments : against the privileges
of regulated companies and corporations, against the
law of apprenticeship, against restrictions on movement,
against restraints on importation. The sense of a
crusade which emerged in the free trade movement
owed some of its force to other, extraneous, influences.
But, up to a point, it is typical of the atmosphere of
the general movement for freeing spontaneous enterprise
and energies of which, without doubt, the Classical Economists were the intellectual spearhead.[1]

---

[1] It may be thought that an exception in this respect should be made for
Malthus, who, as is well known, was not in favour of the free importation of
corn. But too much can be made of this exception. In general, Malthus was at
one with the other Classical Economists in wishing an extensive removal of the
barriers to trade.

(iv) *The Alleged Bias of the Classical Economists*

It is sometimes argued that these ideas are to be regarded essentially as a manifestation of bias. Lord Keynes speaks of the tradition of the Classical Economists as being " marked by a love of truth and a most noble lucidity, by a prosaic sanity free from sentiment or metaphysic, and by an immense disinterestedness and public spirit ".[1] I myself share this view; I find it hard to understand how anyone who has given serious attention to the actual works of these men, however much he may disagree with them, can question their integrity and their transparent devotion to the general good. But this view is not general in our own day. It has become fashionable to dismiss them and their ideas, not on grounds of logic or assumption, but on the grounds of alleged class interest. On this view the Classical Economists are the spokesmen of business, and consciously or unconsciously, the apologists of a dominant class.

Now, it will not be possible to deal conclusively with this question until we have given special attention to the Classical attitude to problems of labour and the condition of the people ; and I do not propose to do this until the third lecture. But at the moment, perhaps, it will help us to understand more thoroughly the spirit of the System of Economic Freedom, if we investigate a little further what Adam Smith actually said about business men and their interests. It may be a bit of a shock to those of you who are acquainted only with contemporary appraisals.

If you look at the chapter on the " Profits of Stock " in the *Wealth of Nations*,[2] you will find that Adam Smith

---

[1] J. M. Keynes, *Essays in Biography*, p. 120.
[2] Adam Smith, *op. cit.* vol. i, p. 89.

took a poor view of the business community as a source
of correct information. " Our merchants and master
manufacturers complain much ", he says, " of the bad
effects of high wages in raising the price, and thereby
lessening the sale of their goods both at home and
abroad. They say nothing concerning the bad effects
of high profits. They are silent with regard to the
pernicious effects of their own gains. They complain
only of those of other people."

Nor does he think that they are to be trusted as
advisers on policy. " To widen the market and to
narrow the competition, is always the interest of the
dealers ", he says. " To widen the market may frequently be agreeable enough to the interest of the
public ; but to narrow the competition must always be
against it, and can serve only to enable the dealers, by
raising their profits above what they naturally would
be, to levy for their own benefit, an absurd tax upon
the rest of their fellow citizens. The proposal of any
new law or regulation of commerce which comes from
this order, ought always to be listened to with great
precaution, and ought never to be adopted till after
having been long and carefully examined, not only with
the most scrupulous, but with the most suspicious attention. It comes from an order of men whose interest is
never exactly the same with that of the public, who have
generally an interest to deceive and even to oppress the
public, and who accordingly have, upon many occasions,
both deceived and oppressed it." [1]

Moreover, he thinks that this influence has had a
peculiarly deleterious influence on the position of the
working classes. " It is the industry which is carried on
for the benefit of the rich and powerful, that is principally
encouraged by our mercantile system. That which is

[1] *Ibid.* vol. i, p. 250.

carried on for the benefit of the poor and the indigent is, too often, either neglected or oppressed." [1]

This is shown further in respect of labour legislation : " Whenever the legislature attempts to regulate the differences between masters and their workmen, its counsellors are always the masters. When the regulation, therefore, is in favour of the workmen it is always just and equitable ; but it is sometimes otherwise when in favour of the masters." [2]

At this stage I will cite only one further example. In a way it is a *curiosum* : yet, nevertheless, it is symptomatic of the degree to which vigilance against class interest was characteristic of this group of men. In the *Constitutional Code*, Bentham devotes some attention to the functions of government regarding public exhibitions and museums. He is in favour of providing drawings of machines and mechanical models : these are of general interest and utility. But he is definitely against public purchases of antique statues, rare books, etc., on the quaint ground that they are only of interest to the rich. " The minds of the rich ", he says, " should not, any more than their bodies, be feasted at the expense of the poor." [3]

(v) *A " Harmonielehre " ?*

For the time being I shall not pursue further this matter of alleged bias ; I shall return to it at length later on.

---

[1] Adam Smith, *op. cit.* vol. ii, p. 143. The whole passage is interesting as an early analysis of monopsonistic exploitation. See also p. 112 for Smith's opinion " how differently the character and conduct of merchants are affected by the high and by the low profits of stock ".

[2] *Ibid.* vol. i, p. 143.

[3] Bentham, *op. cit.* vol. ix, p. 451. If the marshalling of evidence in this connexion were not somewhat otiose, it would be interesting to dwell on Ricardo's proposal for a capital levy for the repayment of war debt. (See Cannan, *The Economic Outlook, Ricardo in Parliament.*) The fact is, of

There is, however, another general criticism of the Classical system which ought to be discussed at this stage : the suggestion that it was essentially theological or mystical, that the claim for economic freedom rested on metaphysical preconceptions of how the world ought to run, rather than on scientific analysis of how it really would run if the conditions assumed were present — the suggestion, in short, that it was what the Germans call a *Harmonielehre*. This is much more interesting than ignorant accusations of class interest ; there is enough of *Harmonielehre* in the occasional terminology of these writers to make the suggestion well worth examining. The simile of the invisible hand gave extensive hostages to superficial criticism.

Let us be clear at the outset concerning the exact issue involved. It is certainly true that the Classical analysis is teleological in the sense that, like all analysis of conduct, it runs in terms of purpose : the purpose of exchange, for instance, is to surrender something which one prefers less to obtain something which one prefers more. But to say this is not to remove it from the sphere of science into the sphere of theology or mysticism. If it were so, much natural science would have to undergo a similar reclassification. To say that legs facilitate bodily motion or that there are certain properties of the blood which, in normal circumstances, act as a safeguard against infection, is not to make any assumption at all concerning the ultimate nature of the world, nor to suggest that the perambulations of a healthy body are always serving some ethically desirable end. The final test whether a statement is metaphysical or scientific is, not whether it includes any assumption of purpose,

course, that the accusations of class interest on the part of the Classical Economists come in the main from a race of people who, if they do not actually know better, do not know because they do not want to know.

but rather whether it argues dogmatically *a priori* or by way of appeal to experience. This means, of course, that in order to remain within the bounds of scientific analysis, the concept of purpose must have a limited sphere of reference.

Now I am prepared to contend that, judged by these tests, the Classical propositions regarding free initiative and the market do not come out too badly. That is not to say that they are ultimately right : that is not what I am investigating. It is only to say that, if what I am about to argue is correct, they are immune from the imputation of mysticism ; they are no mere *Harmonielehre*.

Consider first the mode of their presentation. They are definitely argued, not stated dogmatically. When, for instance, Bentham wishes to demonstrate that the repeal of the usury laws will be conducive to the general interest, he examines the possible repercussions, he considers each typical case on its probable consequences and their merits.[1] He may be right or he may be wrong. But nothing could be further from the theological appeal to the sacred texts or the philosophic appeal to natural law characteristic of the interest controversies of an earlier age. The same is true of Smith's analysis of the function of the market. Common experience is the basis ; each stage of the argument is illustrated by appeal to fact. It is quite true that Adam Smith, who, more than any of the others except Malthus, had certain theological leanings, from time to time clothes his results in the language of Deistic philosophy ; and we know that this has led to misapprehension. But this has no more to do with the fundamental validity of his argument than the theological language in which from time to time Isaac Newton was apt to refer to the universe, had to do with

---

[1] Bentham, *Defence of Usury* : *op. cit.* vol. iii, *passim.*

the validity of his system of natural movements.[1]   In my judgment it is an error to judge the positions adopted in the *Wealth of Nations* by reference back to the *Theory of Moral Sentiments* rather than by examining the merits of the arguments by which they are supported in the contexts in which they appear.

Furthermore, if we examine carefully the extent to which harmony was actually claimed for this system, we shall see that in fact it was very strictly limited. This does not appear from the books about books. But it appears very clearly from the actual texts.

In the first place, it is clear that there was no claim for any harmony at all, if the state did not behave in a certain manner and if certain conditions of the market did not prevail. If the state allowed itself to act in favour of sectional groups or if sectional groups succeeded in forming a monopoly, there was no presumption at all that self-interest was brought into line with the common good. It was realized, moreover, that these dangers were not inconsiderable. " People of the same trade ", said Adam Smith, " seldom meet together, even for merriment and diversion, but the conversation ends in a conspiracy against the public, or in some contrivance to raise prices." [2]   He thought indeed that " It is impossible indeed to prevent such meetings, by any law which either could be executed, or would be consistent

[1] On all this see Professor Viner's essay on " Adam Smith and Laissez-Faire " in the symposium *Adam Smith*, edited by J. M. Clark and published by Chicago University. Professor Viner concludes (pp. 129-130) : " Though Smith in the *Wealth of Nations* frequently makes general statements intended apparently to apply to the entire universe, he has always before him for consideration some concrete problem, or some finite section of the universe. In no instance does Smith rely heavily upon his assertions as to the existence of harmony in the natural order at large to establish his immediate point that such harmony exists within the specific range of economic phenomena which he is at the moment examining." See also W. H. Hutt, *Economists and the Public*, p. 135 *seq.*
[2] Adam Smith, *op. cit.* vol. i, p. 130.

with liberty and justice. But though the law cannot hinder people of the same trade from sometimes assembling together, it ought to do nothing to facilitate such assemblies; much less to render them necessary." And he hoped that under free conditions competition would tend continually to be frustrating their intentions. As we shall see, where it did not have this effect he was not opposed to regulation. It is difficult to see in this very matter-of-fact view any very theological prepossession.

But this is not all. Even granted the establishment of a state of complete economic freedom — an expectation as absurd as the expectation of Oceana or Utopia, according to Adam Smith [1] — the harmony which would be established was a very limited kind of harmony. There would be mutual advantage in exchange : what each party got was worth more to him than what he gave. Given the demand, there would be a rough tendency to appropriate allocation of resources. There would be further a greater stimulus to accumulation and invention, which, because of the pressure of population, were a continuous necessity. But the long-run tendencies of society were not necessarily good at all, nor were the interests of different groups harmonious. The Classical analysis abounds in pessimistic vistas and revelations of clashes of interest.

Thus Adam Smith who believed, as did Malthus in the earlier stages of his thought, that population actually tended to multiply until it pressed on the limits of subsistence, gives a most frightening picture of what may be expected if the funds destined for the maintenance of labour should ever cease to increase. He illustrates this by reference to China where he thought such a dreadful state of affairs actually prevailed.

[1] Adam Smith, *op. cit.* vol. i, p. 435.

" China ", he says, " has been long one of the richest,
that is, one of the most fertile, best cultivated, most
industrious, and most populous countries in the world.
It seems, however, to have been long stationary. . . .
The accounts of all travellers, inconsistent in many other
respects, agree in the low wages of labour, and in the
difficulty which a labourer finds in bringing up a family
in China. If by digging the ground a whole day he can
get what will purchase a small quantity of rice in the
evening, he is contented. The condition of artificers is,
if possible, still worse. Instead of waiting indolently in
their work-houses for the calls of their customers, as in
Europe, they are continually running about the streets
with the tools of their respective trades, offering their
services, and as it were, begging employment. The
poverty of the lower ranks of people in China far sur-
passes that of the most beggarly nations in Europe. In
the neighbourhood of Canton, many hundred, it is
commonly said, many thousand families have no habita-
tion on the land, but live constantly in little fishing
boats upon the rivers and canals. The subsistence which
they find there is so scanty, that they are eager to fish
up the nastiest garbage thrown overboard from any
European ship. Any carrion, the carcase of a dead dog
or cat, for example, though half putrid and stinking, is
as welcome to them as the most wholesome food to the
people of other countries. Marriage is encouraged in
China, not by the profitableness of children, but by the
liberty of destroying them. In all great towns several
are every night exposed in the street, or drowned like
puppies in the water. The performance of this horrid
office is even said to be the avowed business by which
some people earn their subsistence." [1] Only a continuous increase of saving could, he thought, avert such

[1] *Ibid.* vol. i, pp. 73-74.

horrors or even worse. It would be difficult to regard
such a picture as implying any very sanguine view of
the results of the economic process.

The Ricardians were less fatalistic regarding the
tendency of wages to subsistence level ; as we shall see,
later developments of the Malthusian theory had given
some grounds for hope. But they were very apprehensive
lest the stationary state should set in before the working
classes should have had time to learn habits of family
limitation.[1] Moreover, rightly or wrongly, they detected
a sharp conflict in the short run, and possibly in the
long run too, between the interests of the landowners
and other members of society. "They grow richer as
it were in their sleep, without working, risking or eco-
nomizing ", cried J. S. Mill. "What claim have they,
on the general principle of social justice, to this acces-
sion of riches ?"[2] Belief in this particular disharmony
was not shared either by Smith[3] or by Malthus ; but, as
we have just seen, they had their own particular night-
mares.

In general, on any dispassionate view of the literature, it is really very hard to maintain that it gives any
strong support to cosmic optimism, still less to belief in
a comprehensive pre-established inevitable harmony of
interests.[4] The most that can be said of the Classical
Economists in this respect is that they believed that, in
a world of free enterprise, certain relationships would
arise which were of a mutually advantageous kind to the
individuals concerned and superior to those resulting

---

[1] See below, Lecture III.

[2] J. S. Mill, *Principles of Political Economy* (Ashley's edition), p. 818.

[3] Though Adam Smith had pointed out that " the landlords, like all other
men, love to reap where they never sowed ". *Op. cit.* vol. i, p. 51.

[4] From time to time, particularly in the works of Malthus, the existence
of disharmonies is explained by reference to Divine Wisdom. But such reflec-
tions are clearly extraneous to analysis, nor would it be easy to prove that they
had any influence on the theory of policy.

from alternative systems ; and that given certain suitable institutional restraints and state policies (which so far we have left undiscussed) the evil long-run tendencies which they feared might conceivably be arrested, or even eliminated. This may have been right, or it may have been wrong. But it was far from a *Harmonielehre* — at any rate in the pejorative sense of the term.

(vi) *Finance and Automatism*

There was one part of the mechanism of an exchange economy where the claim for even such a limited harmony of interest as I have been just discussing was seldom made in this form ; I refer to the supply of money and credit. For, in the first place, from the time of Hume onwards, it was assumed that the absolute volume of money in existence, as distinct from changes in its volume, was a matter of indifference to the community. Secondly, it was recognized — here, too, the speculations of Hume had put matters into a wide theoretical perspective — that changes in the volume of money might affect production and distribution, with no presumption whatever of general harmony of interest. The history of the discovery of gold and silver in America was not discussed under any presumption that the effects were likely to have been wholly favourable.[1]

Furthermore, we must not suppose that the ups and downs of trade, the financial crises and the economic stagnation which from time to time made their appearance, were a matter of indifference to these economists. As is well known, the explanation was a matter of contention within their ranks. The Ricardians, following

---

[1] D. Hume, *Essays, Moral, Political and Literary* (edited Green and Grose), vol. i, pp. 309 *seq.*

James Mill and J. B. Say,[1] were inclined to attribute the occasional breakdowns of trade to errors of judgment and disproportionate developments of production, while Malthus, in some respects anticipating Keynes — though as through a glass darkly — insisted that they were due to an inappropriate relation between saving and consumption and a sluggishness in the response of the disposition to invest.[2] On the whole at the time, the Ricardians were thought to have had the best of the argument, and the Malthusian arguments fell into neglect. But this is not to say that the general problem ceased to be discussed. The famous controversy between the Currency and the Banking Schools involved much discussion of the vicissitudes of trade. The essay by J. S. Mill on the " Influence of Consumption upon Production " presents the problem debated by Malthus and Ricardo in terms some of which have a surprisingly modern flavour.[3]

The effect of all this in regard to prescriptions of policy is not capable of easy summary. It was readily admitted that here was an area where state action of

[1] James Mill, *Commerce Defended*, pp. 65 *seq.*, chapter vi, "Consumption". *Elements of Political Economy* (3rd edition), chapter iv, section ii, pp. 226 *seq.* J. B. Say, *Traité d'économie politique* (3e édition), t. i, chapter xv, "Des Débouches ", pp. 141 *seq.*, and *Letters to Malthus* (translated London, 1821). See also Ricardo, *Notes on Malthus*, edited Hollander.

[2] Malthus, *Principles of Political Economy* (2nd edition), Book II, chapter i, pp. 309 *seq.* See also J. M. Keynes, *Essays in Biography*, " Robert Malthus ", pp. 138 *seq.* In spite of the high authority of Lord Keynes, I venture to suggest that the more thoroughly Malthus is studied, the more slender appear his claims to be regarded as a precursor of the *General Theory*.

[3] *Essays on Unsettled Questions of Political Economy*, pp. 47-74. For instance : " From what has been already said, it is obvious that periods of ' brisk demand ' are also the periods of greatest production : the national capital is never called into full employment but at these periods. This, however, is no reason for desiring such times : it is not desirable that the whole capital of the country should be in full employment. For the calculations of producers and traders being of necessity imperfect, there are always some commodities which are more or less in excess as there are always some which are in deficiency. If, therefore, the whole truth were known, there would always be some classes of producers contracting, not extending, their operations. If all are endeavouring to extend them, it is a certain proof that some general delusion is afloat " (p. 67.)

some sort was fully justified. Adam Smith goes out of his way to meet objections : " Such regulations ", he says, referring to a proposal for the prohibition of small notes, " may, no doubt, be considered as in some respect a violation of natural liberty. But those exertions of the natural liberty of a few individuals which might endanger the security of the whole society are, and ought to be, restrained by the laws of all governments. . . . The obligation of building party walls, in order to prevent the communication of fire, is a violation of natural liberty, exactly of the same kind with the regulations of the banking trade which are here proposed." [1]

But the form which such regulations should take was not a matter on which there was agreement. The majority of the Classical Economists, distrusting the power of governments to refrain from inflation, were in favour of a metallic currency : there were proposals for managed currencies of the modern kind as early as the period of the restoration of cash payments ; [2] but, with the exception of John Wheatley's second thoughts,[3] they came from outside the group I am discussing. Beyond that, however, there was a division of opinion. On the one hand, Ricardo [4] and the Currency School [5] favoured strict regulation of the note issue, holding that, in the possibility of over-issue, there lay a major danger of over-trading and financial crisis ; no presumption of a universal applicability of the maxim *laissez-faire* seems to have crossed Ricardo's mind as he advocated the

[1] Adam Smith, *op. cit.* vol. i, p. 307. Adam Smith was probably referring to 14 Geo. III, c. 78 — a detailed building code for the London Area.

[2] On this period see Viner, *Studies in the Theory of International Trade*, chapter iv, pp. 171-217.

[3] John Wheatley, *An Essay on the Theory of Money and Principles of Commerce*, vol. ii (1822), pp. 118-145.

[4] Ricardo, *Plan for the Establishment of a National Bank* : *Works* (edited McCulloch), pp. 499-511.

[5] See Overstone, *Works* (edited McCulloch), and Torrens, *Principles and Practical Operation of Sir Robert Peel's Act of 1844* (3rd edition).

nationalization of this function. On the other hand, Tooke and the Banking School,[1] while assuming the desirability of convertibility, favoured free note issue, and argued the supreme necessity of a credit system completely passive to the alleged needs of trade.[2] On these very important matters our Classical predecessors were in something of the same state of divided counsels as we are at the present day.

But, whatever their differences, their attitude to policy in general was not greatly affected. In general, these speculations about money and credit tended to be something of a thing apart. The problem was recognized to be very important ; but the solution, whatever it was, was not conceived to involve other parts of the market mechanism. There was no presumption that a perfect system would arise without a proper framework of law and institutions. But, rightly or wrongly, there was a certain presumption that if anything went wrong with finance it could be put right without modification of arrangements which were thought to be appropriate to other parts of the system. Even Malthus, whose doubts about the social benefits of accumulation and the sluggishness of the disposition to invest might have led him to extremely heterodox attitudes, was very mild and tentative when he came to consider their application to policy : he thought that it was not wise to urge the virtue of saving in all possible contexts ; there was something to be said for the unproductive consumption of the rich ; the benefits of extinction of the National Debt could be over-rated ; sudden changes in demand, due to sudden changes in the tax system, were undesir-

---

[1] See Tooke, *An Inquiry into the Currency Principle*, and Fullarton, *On the Regulation of Currencies*.

[2] On this very interesting phase of the history of thought, consult further Lloyd Mints' *A History of Banking Theory* and Vera Smith's *The Rationale of Central Banking*.

able ; in a depression, there was much to be said for public works which did not get in the way of private enterprise. In the main, however, he was not conspicuously out of step with his fellow Classical Economists, in their theories of the functions of the state.

But what were these theories ? That is the question to which I shall ask you to address your attention in the next lecture.

THE ECONOMIC FUNCTIONS OF THE STATE

(i) *The Popular Mythology*

WE can, perhaps, best approach this task by examining the truth of certain prevalent opinions. I do not think that it is any exaggeration to suggest that to-day, apart from a handful of specialists, the great body of the educated public tends to regard the Classical conception of the functions of the state as sufficiently characterized by Carlyle's phrase, " Anarchy plus the constable ", or by Lassalle's simile of the night watchman. It is this view that I propose to examine.

(ii) *Specimens of Extreme Individualism*

Now I do not question that such conceptions of the functions of the state have been widely held. At most times, in the period under discussion, it would be easy to cull from the political discussions of the day utterances and *obiter dicta* which implied just such an attitude as is suggested by Lassalle's simile. Nor am I prepared to contend that such an attitude is only to be found in the rough-and-tumble of popular controversy. On the contrary, I am clear that it is possible to discover sentiments of this sort on the lips of men who are certainly to be described as economists or social philosophers.

Take, for instance, the alleged conversation between Mercier de La Rivière and Catherine the Great. As you may know, the French economists, the Physiocrats, had a great vogue among the enlightened despots of the eighteenth century. They were invited to the various courts ; their advice was solicited by the great personages. Among those who were thus distinguished was Mercier de La Rivière, the author of *L'Ordre naturel et essentiel des sociétés politiques*, which Adam Smith thought to be the best exposition of the Physiocratic system. He was asked by Catherine the Great to visit Moscow. According to Thiebault, when he arrived, the following conversation took place :

Catherine. " Sir, can you tell me the best way to govern a state ? "

Mercier de La Rivière. " There is only one way, Madame. Be just, that is to say, uphold the constitution and observe the laws."

C. " But on what basis should laws be made ? "

M. " On one basis only, Your Majesty, on the nature of things and of men."

C. " Most certainly. But when one wishes to make these laws what rules should be observed ? "

M. " Madame, to give laws to mankind is God's prerogative. How can mere man venture on such a task ? By what right would he dictate to those whom God has not placed in his hands ? "

C. " To what then do you reduce the science of government ? "

M. " To study the laws which God has so manifestly engraven in human society from the time of its creation. To seek to go beyond this would be a great mistake and a disastrous undertaking."

C. " Sir, it has been a great pleasure to meet you. I wish you good day." [1]

---

[1] *Souvenirs de Berlin* (2nd edition), vol. iii, pp. 167 *seq.* I owe the quotation to Oncken, *Geschichte des Nationalökonomie*, Bd. i, p. 421.

Perhaps this is an over-simplified version of what actually happened ; anecdotes of courts not infrequently tend that way. But no one who has read typical speci- mens of the Physiocratic literature would contend that it was altogether out of character.

Or take Bastiat. In his *Harmonies économiques* he lays it down that " It is the essence of government that it acts on the citizens by way of constraint. Therefore it cannot have any other rational function but the legiti- mate defence of individual rights, it has no authority but to make respected the liberties and the properties of all. . . . Beyond justice, I challenge anyone to imagine a governmental intervention which is not an injustice. . . . Thus : to preserve the public security : to ad- minister the common domain [Rivers, Forests, Roads], to impose taxes ; here, I believe, is the rational circle within which the function of government must be circumscribed or restricted. . . ." [1]

The attitude of Herbert Spencer in *Man versus the State* is of a similar order of simplicity. Of course, the object of this famous polemic is chiefly negative : the author is arguing against a trend of policy ; and it is a common habit in such circumstances to tend to overstate the case. Nevertheless, it is certainly not un- fair to depict him as opposed on principle to state regulation concerning health, safety and compulsory education. The regulations themselves, he argues, are usually pernicious ; and the cumulative tendency is towards the servile state.

(iii) *The Classical Theory*

Thus there can be no doubt that doctrines as extreme as those pilloried by Carlyle and Lassalle have had

---

[1] Bastiat, *Œuvres complètes* (1864), vol. vi, pp. 553-555.

extensive currency and the support of famous names. But they did not have the support of the Classical Economists. To identify such doctrines with the declared and easily accessible views of the Classical Economists is a sure sign of ignorance or malice. This is a strong statement, which must be supported by extensive evidence.

According to Adam Smith, the state has three functions, " first, the duty of protecting the society from the violence and invasion of other independent societies ; secondly, the duty of protecting, as far as possible, every member of the society from the injustice or oppression of every other member of it ; and, thirdly, [note the wording here] the duty of erecting and maintaining certain public works and certain public institutions, which it can never be for the interest of any individual, or small number of individuals, to erect and maintain ; because the profit could never repay the expense to any individual or small number of individuals, though it may frequently do much more than repay it to a great society ".[1]

Before we go any further, it is interesting to compare this formulation of the functions of the state with the formulation which we find in Keynes' celebrated pamphlet *The End of Laissez-Faire*. " The most important *Agenda* of the state ", says Keynes, following Bentham's terminology, " relate not to those activities which private individuals are already fulfilling, but to those functions [please note the wording again] which fall outside the sphere of the individual, to those decisions which are made by *no one* if the State does not make them. The important thing for Government is not to do things which individuals are doing already, and to do them a little better or a little worse ; but to do those things which at present are not done at all." [2]

[1] Adam Smith, *op. cit.* vol. ii, pp. 184-185.   [2] *Supra*, pp. 46-47.

It would, of course, be misleading to suggest that the *content* of Lord Keynes' *agenda* was identical with that of Adam Smith's — control of aggregate investment and policy designed to affect the size and quality of the population were conspicuous among his illustrations — and it is quite clear that such were alien to Adam Smith's conception. But the *formal* similarity is not an accident ; it indicates the essential continuity of thought in the tradition of economic liberalism concerning the positive nature of the co-operation between the state and the individual. Nor must we regard the content of Adam Smith's *agenda* as limited to provision of roads, canals, harbours and such like utilities. As we shall see, he made a most powerful plea for popular education and he indicated that, had he known of any available technique, he would have favoured health legislation.[1]

For the rest, we have already seen that he laid it down as a principle that those exertions of the natural liberty of a few individuals which might endanger the whole society ought to be restrained ;[2] and a careful reading of the *Wealth of Nations* will yield a very substantial number of illustrations, from quality certificates for linen and woollen cloth[3] and regulations concerning land settlement in new countries,[4] to the control of the price of bread if the supply is in the hands of a monopoly.[5] I have no desire to present a paradoxical picture of Smith as an enlightened interventionist. That would be a false perspective. But the perspective is no less false which presents him as one who would reduce the functions of the state to those of the night watchman.

I pass next to Bentham, whose significance as pro-

---

[1] Adam Smith, *op. cit.* vol. ii, p. 272 : ". . . It would deserve its most serious attention to prevent a leprosy or any other loathsome and offensive disease, though neither mortal nor dangerous from spreading itself. . . ."

[2] See Lecture I above, p. 31.   [3] *Op. cit.* vol. i, p. 124.

[4] *Ibid.* vol. ii, pp. 73-74.   [5] *Ibid.* vol. i, p. 144.

viding the philosophical background for the later developments has not, I think, always been fully appreciated by
historians of economic thought. It is, of course, well
known that he was the founder of the sect of more rigid
Utilitarians, and, in his later days, active in the propaganda of the Philosophical Radicals. But, quite as important as the general statement of the greatest happiness
principle was its detailed working out in relation to law
and institutions : it is here, I fancy, that the importance
of Bentham's work in regard to economic policy has not
always been sufficiently understood.

If we look at the passage which I read last time, re-
calling Diogenes' request to Alexander, or if we read the
famous *Be quiet* injunction to government which is also
to be found in the first chapter of the *Manual of Political
Economy*, we may easily be tempted to put Bentham
among the extreme exponents of a negative view of state
function. It was doubtless these passages which led
Lord Keynes, who himself had pre-eminently the *flair*
for the striking phrase, in a momentary fit of absence of
mind to put Bentham in his gallery of extreme partisans
of this doctrine.[1] If, however, we are prepared to read
the whole book, still more to consider Bentham's work
as a whole, the impression that emerges is decidedly
different.

In the first place, as Professor Viner has recently
reminded us,[2] we observe that the *agenda* differ according
to historical circumstances. " The distribution of the
imaginable stock of institutions [*i.e.* among *agenda*,
sponte acta and *non agenda*] will in a very considerable
degree differ according to the different circumstances
of the several political communities. . . . In England

---

[1] Keynes, *op. cit.* p. 21.
[2] See his Address to the American Economic Association, " Bentham and
J. S. Mill : the Utilitarian Background ", *American Economic Review*, March
1949.

abundance of useful things are done by individuals, which in other countries are done either by governments or not at all. . . . In Russia, under Peter the Great, the list of *sponte acta* being a blank, that of *agenda* was proportionately abundant." [1] This might perhaps be noted by those who, with the German Historical School, are always arguing that the Utilitarians were not " historically-minded ".[2]

Secondly, we must observe that although there is an explicit presumption that, over a wide field, interference is inadvisable, there is no suggestion that it is ruled out *a priori* by some system of natural rights. Bentham had no use whatever for the *Naturrecht*, and he continually goes out of his way to make this clear. Thus he is most contemptuous about those who would argue that because taxation involves a burden on those who pay it, therefore, it should be avoided. " It would . . . be a gross error, and an extremely mischievous one, to refer to the defalcation thus resulting from the mass of liberty or free agency, as affording a conclusive objection against the inter-position of the law for this or any other purpose. Every law which does not consist in the repeal, total or partial, of a coercive law, is itself a coercive law. To reprobate as a mischief resulting from this or that law, a property which is the essence of all law, is to betray . . . a total unacquaintance with what may be called the logic of the laws." [3] According to the principle of

[1] Bentham, *op. cit.* vol. iii, p. 35, footnote. See also the separate work on the *Influence of Time and Place in Matters of Legislation* : *op. cit.* vol. i, pp. 169, 194.

[2] It must not, however, be regarded as a proof that Bentham was a precursor of Schmoller. To take account of the influence of place and time in applying general principles is not to proclaim the degrading mystique of historicism. .

[3] Bentham, *op. cit.* vol. iii, pp. 34, 70. " In recommending freedom of trade, I suppose the minds of merchants in their sound, that is, their ordinary state. But there have been times when they acted as though they were delirious: such were the period of the Mississippi Scheme in France and the South Sea

utility, as distinct from the *Naturrecht*, the expediency of any act of government must be judged solely by its consequences and not regarded as ruled out in advance by some metaphysical system of rights. In fact, even in the *Manual* we find the most surprising examples of state action which is said to be beneficial — from accumulation, for instance, of large stocks of food against famine in circumstances where the private market does not function adequately in this respect,[1] to intervention to prevent over-speculation in stock markets.[2] He has, moreover, Adam Smith's formal argument regarding institutions involving indiscriminate benefit, illustrated *inter alia* by a justification of the building of the Caledonian Canal which might easily come from a modern work dilating on the arcana of the doctrine of external economies — though it has not the same esoteric air.[3] In a letter written as early as 1776, we find a clear exposition of the desirability of public works as a means of relieving unemployment.[4]

But I shall give a false impression if I restrict myself to piquant examples. You get Bentham quite out of perspective if you do not think of him essentially as the great legal inventor, the greatest perhaps in history, continually seeking all along the line to erect a structure of institutions, thought out in great detail, within which action is so limited and co-ordinated as to create the

Scheme in England. The other classes of people would have had ground for seeking to divert their fellow citizens from the purchase of the smoke sold by Law, or of the *bubbles* of the South Sea."

[1] *Ibid.* p. 71.   [2] *Ibid.* p. 71.

[3] " The justification of the communication from sea to sea through Scotland by the Caledonian Canal, is to be sought for in the same principles, though the preponderance of profit over expense can scarcely be expected to prove equally considerable. Of the profit part, though to an unassignable amount will distribute itself among a limited, and perhaps individually assignable description of individuals : other part, in portions altogether unassignable, among individuals more clearly assignable ; viz. among the community at large." *Ibid.* p. 41, note.

[4] Bentham, *op. cit.* vol. x, p. 85.

good society. I wonder how many now living have ever opened the *Constitutional Code*, the great project for a practical Utopia on which Bentham lavished so much of the care and emotion of the final years of his life. Those who do, even if they restrict themselves only to the contents table, must find a picture which squares very ill with the contemporary idea of the *laissez-faire* state. Let me quote the Bentham cabinet : besides the Prime Minister :—

> Election Minister.
> Legislation Minister.
> Army Minister.
> Navy Minister.
> Preventive Service Minister (Police, Fire, etc.).
> Interior Communication Minister.
> Indigence Relief Minister.
> Education Minister.
> Domain Minister.
> Health Minister.
> Foreign Relations Minister.
> Trade Minister.
> Finance Minister.[1]

Pretty comprehensive is it not ? When we look into the detail of the arrangements we note that care has been taken to provide a Central Statistical Office (" statistic function "), a competitively selected Civil Service, and many other administrative arrangements hardly achieved even at the present day. Among the instructions to the President of the Board of Trade is one that he is to bear in mind the need for continual revision of regulations involved by the " effect produced on the money prices of commodities — things movable and immovable — by variations in the relative aggregate quantity of money

---

[1] Bentham, *op. cit.* vol. ix, p. 7.

of various sorts, as compared with the aggregate quantity of commodities destined for sale ". I confess that when I find this sort of thing I feel that, in some respects at any rate, modern practice has yet some little distance to go before it catches up with Jeremy Bentham.[1]

I must not prolong unduly this procession of witnesses. But we must not restrict ourselves to the founders : it might be argued that there had been some departure from these standards in the second and third generations. As is well known, Mill in his *Principles* devoted a whole book (Book V) to the province of government, which abounds in illustrations of what I am trying to demonstrate. But I shall be referring sufficiently to Mill later on ; and at this stage it might be thought that his attitude was untypical. I prefer therefore to rely on McCulloch and Senior, of whom, on popular estimates, less of this sort of thing is to be expected.

McCulloch has a systematic discussion of the functions of government in his *Principles*. This embraces a wide field of the kind that we should expect in one who had read Smith and Bentham, and includes a strong plea for the statutory limitation of the dividends of public utility organizations. In his treatise on inheritance we may note a striking, though not untypical, repudiation of the principle of *laissez-faire*. " The principle of *laissez-faire* may be safely trusted to in some things but in many more it is wholly inapplicable ; and to appeal to it on all occasions savours more of the policy of a parrot than of a statesman or a philosopher." [2]

---

[1] *Ibid.* p. 447.

[2] J. R. McCulloch, *Treatise on the Succession to Property Vacant by Death* (1848), p. 156. In his thought-provoking book on *Economic Thought and Policy*, p. 54, Professor Macgregor suggests, as evidence of their lack of commitment to this principle, that " the English Classical Economists did not use this phrase at all, until Mill pronounced it a rule of general practice in 1848 ". While accepting completely Professor Macgregor's general position as regards the attitude of the English Classical Economists and his view that extensive use of

Even more remarkable, however, are the remarks in the preface to his *Principles*. " It may, for example, be laid down as a general rule that the more individuals are thrown on their own resources, and the less they are taught to rely on extrinsic and adventitious assistance, the more industrious and economical will they become, and the greater, consequently, will be the amount of public wealth. But, even in mechanics, the engineer must allow for the friction and resistance of matter ; and it is still more necessary that the economist should make a corresponding allowance, seeing that he has to deal not only with natural powers, but with human beings enjoying political privileges, and imbued with the strongest feelings, passions and prejudices. Although, therefore, the general principle as to self-reliance be as stated above, the economist or the politician who should propose carrying it out to its full extent in all cases and at all hazards, would be fitter for bedlam than for the closet or the cabinet. When any great number of work-

the term *laissez-faire* comes after rather than before 1848, I cannot help thinking that his assertion regarding its total absence from the pre-1848 literature is a little too strong. Apart from the quotation from McCulloch given above, in reading preparatory to the writing of these lectures I have also found it in vol. ii of Wheatley's *Theory of Money* (p. 199), in a letter from J. S. Mill to Carlyle in 1833 (*Letters of John Stuart Mill* (edited Hugh Elliot), vol. i, p. 46), and in Torrens' *Letter to Lord Ashley* (1844) (p. 64), and I feel pretty sure that a systematic search would reveal further examples. It is to be noted that, apart from Wheatley's, these allusions occur in passages repudiating the principle, thus sustaining Professor Macgregor's main contention. Mill says, " Your criticism of Miss Martineau is, I think, just ; she reduces the *laissez-faire* system to absurdity as far as the principle goes, by merely carrying it out to all its consequences. In the meantime that principle, like other negative ones, has work to do yet, namely work of a destroying kind, and I am glad to think it has strength left to finish that, after which it must still soon expire : peace be with its ashes when it does expire, for I doubt much whether it will reach the resurrection." Torrens anticipates McCulloch in the simile of the parrot : " In the majority of instances in which it is put forth, the maxim of *laissez-faire* is an imitative sound, repeated with as little effort of discriminating thought as that which distinguishes ' The coxcomb bird so talkative and grave ' ". Torrens had perhaps some reason to make his position explicit in this respect, for there are passages in his *Essay on the Production of Wealth*, written twenty years earlier, which might easily be made the basis of adherence to the principle.

people are thrown out of employment, they must be provided for by extraneous assistance in one way or other ; so that the various questions with respect to a voluntary and compulsory provision for the destitute poor, are as necessary parts of this science as the theories of rent and of profit."

Senior is even stronger. In his anonymous review of Mill in the *Edinburgh Review* in 1848 he poses the question, " Is it true that governments ought to confine themselves to affording protection against force and fraud ? ", and comes to the conclusion that the arguments in favour of this principle " cannot be supported ". He even takes exception to Mill's use of the term " optional " as applied to the function of government. " Like the words ' boon ' or ' concession ', it seems to imply that there may be useful measures which the government of a country may at its discretion adopt or reject." [1] And in his Oxford lectures of 1847–48 he lays it down that " the only rational foundation of government, the only foundation of a right to govern and a correlative duty to obey is, expediency — the general benefit of the community. It is the duty of a government to do whatever is conducive to the welfare of the governed. The only limit to this duty is power . . . it appears to me that the most fatal of all errors would be the general admission of the proposition that· a government has no right to interfere for any purpose except for that of affording protection, for such an admission would be preventing our profiting by experience, and even from acquiring it." [2]

Unless words of this sort are to be taken as deliberate

---

[1] J. S. Mill's *Political Economy*: *Edinburgh Review*, October 1848, vol. clxxviii, p. 294 *seq.*

[2] This lecture has never been published in its original form. But a snippet is given in the compilation of extracts from Senior's published and unpublished works entitled *Industrial Efficiency and Social Economy* (edited S. Leon Levy), vol. ii, p. 302.

deception, they must surely be regarded as conclusive evidence against the attribution to those who used them of the night-watchman theory of the functions of government.

(iv) *" Naturrecht "* and *Utility*

But, if this is so, we are confronted with a nice historical problem. The great individualist movement of the eighteenth and nineteenth centuries is seen to rest not on one but on two different points of view. On the one hand, you have those who, like Mercier de La Rivière and Bastiat, conceive the system of economic freedom arising spontaneously in a *milieu* in which the functions of the state are minimal and more or less cut and dried for all times and all places. On the other hand, you have the English Classical School who, while urging just as strongly the claim for the freeing of trade and enterprise, conceive the functions of the state in a much more positive and experimental spirit and who are not prepared to lay down in advance prohibitions of state action resting on conceptions of a natural order of things at once simple and universally applicable. These two groups are at one in their protest against Mercantilism. But in their general theories of society they proceed on divergent lines. Why was this ?

It is tempting, I think, to attribute some of the difference to difference of context and plane of argument : it is reasonable to suppose that some at least of the negative emphasis of extreme individualism is the by-product of the controversial setting. In polemical discussion there is a tendency to over-emphasis ; if you are arguing against fatuous regulations you do not necessarily feel under any immediate obligation to state all that you would really agree to be desirable functions of government. There are many *obiter dicta*, even in the Classical literature, which clearly call for this interpretation.[1]

But this is not all ; the difference goes much deeper than that. As I see it, liberal theories of economic policy in the eighteenth and nineteenth centuries spring from two distinct philosophical origins. On the one hand, you have the tradition of natural law and natural rights, according to which the criterion of policy consists essentially of conformity to a pre-established natural order capable of very easy definition and invariant in time and space — *" rien de plus simple, ni de plus évident que les principes fondamentaux et invariables de l'ordre naturel et essentiel des sociétés "*, said Mercier de La Rivière.[2] On the other hand, you have the Utilitarian tradition, influential conspicuously through Hume and Bentham, according to which all laws and rights were to be regarded as essentially man-made and to be evaluated according to their effects on the general happiness, long term and short. The one is typified by Quesnai's motto for the title-page of Du Pont's *Physiocratie*,

Ex natura, jus, ordo, et leges
Ex homine, arbitrium, regimen, et coercitio.

The other by Bentham's description of natural rights as " simple nonsense, natural and imprescriptible rights,

[1] Thus, for instance, on p. 98 of their Report on the Handloom Weavers, the Commissioners remark : " We believe in short that . . . the duty of government is simply to keep the peace, to protect all its subjects from the violence, and fraud and malice of one another, and having done so, to leave them to pursue their interests in the way which they deem advisable ". But it would be a great mistake to infer from this a *laissez-faire* attitude, in the sense of the popular histories of economic thought. For earlier in the report there are strong pleas for housing regulation and popular education. See Lecture III, below.

[2] Mercier de La Rivière, *L'Ordre naturel et essentiel des sociétés politiques, collection des économistes* (1910), p. 30.

rhetorical nonsense — nonsense upon stilts ".[1]

It is possible, of course, to draw the contrast too strongly. Life is not consistent and influences are mixed. This can well be seen in Adam Smith, who so frequently uses the terminology of the *Naturrecht*, but whose arguments are so consistently utilitarian in character ; and I am prepared to concede to Professor Gonnard that the empirical and utilitarian point of view is "far from being absent "[2] from the Physiocrats. But, broadly speaking, the difference exists and is significant. It is surely very significant that when Cairnes felt called upon to deliver a frontal attack on the attempt to associate political economy with a dogmatic *laissez-faire*, he should have chosen Bastiat as his target, for Bastiat could hardly write about anything without invoking the idea of natural rights.[3] And I suggest that it is no accident that when Herbert Spencer, in his apprehension of collectivism, put forward what is probably the most uncompromising and extreme individualism in the whole literature of English political philosophy, he should have thought it desirable to couple this with a denunciation of Benthamite utilitarianism and an attempt

[1] Bentham, *Anarchical Fallacies* : *op. cit.* vol. ii, p. 501. The contrast is explicitly recognized by John Stuart Mill in his essay on Comte (*August Comte and Positivism*, pp. 69-73). See also A. Schatz, *Individualisme, économique et social*, especially pp. 113-147. But nowhere perhaps is it more clearly put than by David Buchanan, the first editor of the *Wealth of Nations*, when, contrasting the work of the Physiocrats with that of Adam Smith, he says, " It may also be remarked of the French authors that however consistently they maintain the doctrine of the freedom of trade, they seem to deduce it from the principles rather of abstract right, than of general expediency ". (*Wealth of Nations*, edited Buchanan, 1814, vol. i, p. vi.) He goes on to remark that, " In proving their doctrines to be just rather than expedient, the French writers are . . . excluded from all those practical views of society and of manners, which render science so much more certain and interesting, by bringing it home to the business of life."

[2] R. Gonnard, *Histoire des doctrines économiques*, vol. ii, p. 100, note. For instance, M. de La Rivière managed to bring the desirability of some public education into the framework of the Natural and Essential Order.

[3] Cairnes, *Essays in Political Economy* : Essay VII, " Political Economy and Laissez-Faire ", and Essay IX, " Bastiat ".

to rehabilitate, *via* his particular theory of evolution, the antithetical theory of the system of natural rights.[1]

(v) *The Theory of Property*

We can see the nature of the contrast I am trying to establish if we proceed one stage further on our way and examine the different conceptions of property in these different schools of thought.

As we have seen, Mercier de La Rivière found "nothing simpler, nothing more evident than the natural and essential order of society". This insight enabled him to see without difficulty the rationale of the institution of property.

"Here then is absolute justice", he says. " This is how it presents itself to us in all its simplicity : once we perceive the physical necessity which obliges us to live in society, we perceive that it is also a necessity, and consequently absolute justice, that each man should be exclusive proprietor of his person and of the things which he acquires by his researches and his work. We perceive too that it is a necessity and absolute justice that each man should respect the property rights of others ",[2] and he goes on to say that " if anyone should make any difficulty about recognizing the natural and essential order of society as a branch of physical [*sic*] necessity, I should regard him as deliberately blind and I should not trouble to attempt to cure him ".[3]

Let us now turn to David Hume. We know that Hume had not much use for the Physiocrats : in a letter to Morellet he describes them as a set of men " the

---

[1] Herbert Spencer, *Man versus the State,* especially the section entitled " The Great Political Superstition ".

[2] Mercier de La Rivière, *op. cit.* p. 10.

[3] *Ibid.* pp. 28-29.

most chimerical and most arrogant that now exist " ; [1]
and if we compare his treatment of property in the
Enquiry Concerning the Principles of Morals [2] with
Mercier de La Rivière's, we should not find it hard to see
the temperamental and intellectual grounds of difference.
This treatment must surely be regarded as one of the
high points of speculative achievement in the sphere of
moral science ; and, since it is much less well known than
it deserves to be,[3] I propose to quote it at some length.

Hume begins by stating bluntly that public utility is
the sole origin of justice (*i.e.* the law regarding property).
The contrast with the outlook of the *Naturrecht* could not
be more baldly stated.

He then goes on to consider various conditions in
which the institution of property would not be necessary.
First, he supposes a state of " such profuse *abundance* of
all *external* conveniences that, without any uncertainty
in the event, without any care or industry on our part,
every individual finds himself fully provided with whatever his most voracious appetites can want, or luxurious
imagination desire ".[4] In such a state of affairs " the
cautious, jealous virtue of justice would never once have
been dreamed of . . . why give rise to property when
there cannot possibly be any injury ? Why call this

---

[1] Hume, *Letters* (edited Greig), vol. ii, p. 205. Morellet himself was pretty
simpliste. In a letter to Shelburne he expresses himself as follows : " Since
liberty is a natural state, and restrictions are on the contrary, the state of
compulsion, by giving back liberty everything reassumes its own place and
everything is at peace provided only that thieves and murderers continue to be
caught " (*Lettres de l'abbé Morellet à Lord Shelburne*, p. 102).

[2] David Hume, *Essays, Moral, Political and Literary* (edited Green and
Grose), vol. ii, p. 179 *seq.* An earlier version of this theory is to be found in the
Treatise on Human Nature, Book III, part ii, sections i-v. But the exposition
of the *Enquiry* is undoubtedly superior. It reproduces the earlier arguments
but with incomparably greater force. It is easy to understand why Hume was
so pleased with this work.

[3] But see the important article by Professor Sir Arnold Plant on *The
Economic Theory concerning Patents for Inventions* (*Economica*, February 1934,
p. 30 *seq.*).

[4] Hume, *op. cit.* p. 179.

object *mine*, when upon the seizing it by another, I need but stretch out my hand to possess myself of what is equally valuable. . . . Even in the present necessitous condition of mankind, that, whenever any benefit is bestowed by nature in an unlimited abundance, we leave it always in common among the whole human race, and make no subdivisions of right and property." [1]

Secondly, he supposes a state in which customary scarcities prevail but in which " the mind is so enlarged, and so replete with friendship and generosity, that every man has the utmost tenderness for every man, and feels no more concern for his own interest than for that of his fellows ".[2] In such a case there would be no use for property. " Why raise landmarks between my neighbour's field and mine, when my heart has made no division between our interests ; but shares all his joys and sorrows with the same force and vivacity as if originally my own. . . . The whole human race would form only one family ; where all would lie in common, and be used freely, without regard to property." [3] He thinks examples of such a state of affairs are hard to find on a large scale, but that, to some extent, it actually prevails within the family.

Then he reverses the first supposition and supposes a condition of siege. Clearly all regard for property breaks down. Even in less urgent circumstances, the public " opens granaries without the consent of proprietors ; as justly supposing that the authority of magistracy may, consistent with equity, extend so far ".[4] Moreover, if a man falls into the hands of ruffians or, if a civilized nation is at war with barbarians, regard for property ceases.

Thus, he concludes, the argument that the justification of property is utility is vindicated. " The common

[1] *Ibid.* p. 180.   [2] *Ibid.* p. 181.   [3] *Ibid.* p. 182.   [4] *Ibid.* p. 180.

situation of mankind is a medium amidst all these extremes. We are naturally partial to ourselves, and to our friends ; but are capable of learning the advantage resulting from a more equitable conduct. Few enjoyments are given us from the open and liberal hand of nature ; but by art, labour, and industry, we can extract them in great abundance. Hence the ideas of property become necessary in all civil society : Hence justice derives its usefulness to the public : And hence alone arises its merit and moral obligation." [1]

He then goes on to ask how property should be distributed. He dismisses the principle that the largest possessions should go to the most extensive virtue. " In a perfect theocracy, where a being, infinitely intelligent, governs by particular volitions, this rule would certainly have place and might serve the wisest purposes : But were mankind to execute such a law ; so great is the uncertainty of merit, both from its natural obscurity and from the self-conceit of each individual, that no determinate rule would ever result from it ; and the total dissolution of society must be the immediate consequence." [2]

He pays much more attention to the principle of equality. He thinks that there is enough to go round on this basis and to maintain a fair standard of comfort. He also confesses that " wherever we depart from this equality, we rob the poor of more satisfaction than we add to the rich, and that the slight gratification of a frivolous vanity in one individual, frequently costs more than bread to many families, and even provinces ". But egalitarian distribution will not work. " Historians and even commonsense, may inform us, that, however specious these ideas of perfect equality may *seem*, they are really, at bottom, *impracticable*, and were they not

---

[1] Hume, *op. cit.* vol. ii, p. 183.   [2] *Ibid.* p. 187.

so, would be extremely *pernicious* to human society. Render possessions ever so equal, men's different degrees of art, care and industry will immediately break that equality. Or if you check these virtues, you reduce society to the most extreme indigence ; and instead of preventing want and beggary in a few, render it unavoidable to the whole community." [1]   Moreover, it would need a most vigorous inquisition to watch every inequality on its first appearance and " so much authority must soon degenerate into tyranny ".

Hence considerations of utility suggest the general desirability of property, inheritance and the enforcement of contracts. " Who sees not, for instance, that whatever is produced or improved by man's art or industry ought, for ever, to be secured to him, in order to give encouragement to such *useful* habits and accomplishments ? That the property ought also to descend to children and relations, for the same *useful* purpose ? That it may be alienated by consent, in order to beget that commerce and intercourse which is so *beneficial* to human society ? And that all contracts and promises ought carefully to be fulfilled, in order to secure mutual trust and confidence, by which the general *interest* of mankind is so much promoted." Even writers on natural law, when they get off their high horse, come down to this. " What other reason, indeed, could writers ever give why this must be *mine* and that *yours* ; since uninstructed nature, surely, never made any such distinction. The objects which receive these appellations, are, of themselves, foreign to us : they are totally disjointed and separated from us ; and nothing but the general interests of society can form the connection." [2]

He then goes on to expatiate on the extremely

[1] *Ibid.* p. 188.   [2] *Ibid.* p. 189.

artificial nature of the law. " Sometimes the interests of
society may require a rule of justice in a particular case,
but may not determine any particular rule, among
several, which are all equally beneficial. In that case,
the *slightest* analogies are laid hold of, in order to prevent
that indifference and ambiguity, which would be the
source of perpetual dissension. Thus possession alone,
and first possession, is supposed to convey property,
where nobody else has any preceding claim and pre-
tension." [1] Sometimes the decision has to be arbitrary.
" It is highly requisite, that prescription or long possession should convey property : but what number of
days or months or years should be sufficient for that
purpose, it is impossible for reason alone to determine." [2]
Thus to establish what is a man's property it is necessary
to " have recourse to statutes, customs, precedents and
analogies, and a hundred other circumstances, some of
which are constant and inflexible, some variable and
arbitrary ".[3] But " the ultimate point in which they all
professedly terminate " and the ultimate justification
for maintaining them must be " the interest and happiness of human society ". Were it not for this they
would be on the same footing as superstitions which make
some foods lawful to some, unlawful to others. " Were
the interests of society nowise concerned, it is as un-
intelligible, why another's articulating certain sounds
implying consent, should change the nature of any
actions with regard to a particular object, as why the
reciting of a liturgy by a priest, in a certain habit and
posture, should dedicate a heap of brick and timber,
and render it, thenceforth and forever, sacred." [4]

Finally, he scoffs at the idea that " property, which
is the object of justice, is also distinguished by a simple

[1] Hume, *op. cit.* p. 189.   [2] *Ibid.* p. 190.
[3] *Ibid.* p. 191.   [4] *Ibid.* p. 193.

original instinct ". In fact, " there are required for that purpose ten thousand different instincts, and these employed about objects of the greatest intricacy and nicest discernment. For when a definition of property is required, that relation is found to resolve itself into any possession acquired by occupation, by industry, by prescription, by inheritance, by contract, etc. Can we think, that nature, by an original instinct instructs us in all these methods of acquisition ? . . . These words, too, inheritance and contract, stand for ideas infinitely complicated ; and to define them exactly a hundred volumes of laws, and a thousand volumes of commentators, have not been found sufficient. Does nature, whose instincts in men are all simple, embrace such complicated and artificial objects, and create a rational creature, without trusting anything to the operation of his reason ? " [1]

(vi) *State Action and the System of Economic Freedom*

I hope that by now there is beginning to emerge a general picture of the Classical theory of the desirable social order — of the relation between their conception of the functions of the state and the System of Economic Freedom.

On this view the good society is to be regarded as an artifact. For the Classical Economists, as for Locke, the state of nature is a poor business. They do not

[1] *Ibid.* pp. 194-195. Considerations of space and proportion forbid a detailed following up of the development of the Classical theory of property. The treatment by Bentham in his *Principles of the Civil Code* : *op. cit.* vol. i, pp. 308-311, 326-338, and John Stuart Mill in his *Principles of Political Economy*, Book II, chapter i, are especially deserving of attention. It is to be observed that on the principle of limited liability the Classical writers were divided, McCulloch, Tooke and Overstone being opposed, J. S. Mill and Norman being in favour. See B. C. Hunt's *Development of the Business Corporation in England*, especially pp. 117, 121, 125-127.

believe in an original contract ; Hume made eternal fun
of that fiction.[1] They do not believe that all beneficial
social activities have been planned from the centre, nor
that it is desirable that planning of this detailed sort
should be attempted.   But they do believe in the
conscious testing of all social institutions by the general
principle of utility.   And they do believe that without
a firm framework of law and order, harmonious relations
between individuals are unlikely to come into being ;
the pursuit of self-interest, unrestrained by suitable
institutions, carries no guarantee of anything except
chaos.   Moreover, these institutions are not natural in
the sense that they arise inevitably.   They can only be
called natural if by that word is meant conformable to
the principle of utility ; and while they may emerge
without deliberate reflection on all their implications,
their fitness to survive must be judged by rational
criteria.

Thus, so far from the system of economic freedom
being something which will certainly come into being if
things are just left to take their course, it can only come
into being if they are *not* left to take their course, if a
conscious effort is made to create the highly artificial
environment which is necessary if it is to function
properly.   The invisible hand which guides men to
promote ends which were no part of their intention, is
not the hand of some god or some natural agency independent of human effort ; it is the hand of the law-
giver, the hand which withdraws from the sphere of the
pursuit of self-interest those possibilities which do not
harmonize with the public good.   There is absolutely no
suggestion that the market can furnish everything ; on
the contrary, it can only begin to furnish anything when
a whole host of other things have been furnished another

---

[1] Hume, *op. cit.* vol. i, " On the Original Contract ", p. 443 *seq.*

way. It is not only the special services yielding indiscriminate benefit which fall outside its function, it is also
the whole fabric of law without which it could not exist.
Without Hume's theory of justice, or something very
much like it, the Classical theory of self-interest and the
market would remain completely in the air. Not only
the good society, but the market itself is an artifact.

It is necessary to emphasize all this in order to point
the contrast between the Classical and other libertarian
systems — the anarchical system which assumes no need
for law and order at all and the *naturrechtlich* systems
which indeed assume the necessity for some such
apparatus, but assume it to be so simple that it can be
deduced from revelation or the principles of pure reason
and written on half a sheet of notepaper.

But the fact that a mechanism is artificial does not
mean that it can be made to do anything. A steam
engine is artificial ; but its working is still governed by
the facts of its construction. And it was the central contention of the Classical Economists that, when the
market conformed to the conditions which they postulated, then interference with its working was harmful and
self-frustrating. They did not conceive the self-acting
mechanism to be self-created. But they did conceive
that once it had been so conditioned as to conform to their
idea of what was self-acting, then it was not merely
superfluous but positively pernicious to attempt to use
other coercive influences.

We can trace this attitude both in their prohibitions
and their occasional exceptions.

They were against price-fixing. Assuming that competition was free, they were against both upper and
lower limits on prices.

But, if there was no competition, this prohibition did
not necessarily hold. It is true that they were inclined

to argue that if supply positions were not licensed or made the subject of exceptional privilege, then competition would prevail. But, if this were not so, the presumption against price-fixing ceased to be operative. I have mentioned that Adam Smith was prepared to control the price of bread if the supply was in the hands of a monopoly and that McCulloch was in favour of the limitation of the dividends of public utility companies. John Stuart Mill said of public utilities in general that " a government which concedes such monopoly unreservedly to a private company does much the same thing as if it allowed an individual or an association to levy any tax they chose, for their own benefit, on all the malt produced in the country or on all the cotton imported into it. To make the concession for a limited time is generally justifiable, on the principle which justifies patents for inventions : but the state should either reserve to itself a reversionary property in such public works, or should retain, and freely exercise, the right of fixing a maximum of fares and charges, and, from time to time, varying that maximum." [1]

In the same way, if we turn from prices to the volume of supply, we find that they were opposed to attempts to produce alterations by taxes or bounties. There were exceptions for defence industries. But it was the essence of the doctrine of self-interest and the market that, provided the situation was competitive, interference designed to make the supply different from what it otherwise would have been was ill-advised.

They did not think that interference was necessarily

---

[1] J. S. Mill, *Principles of Political Economy* (Ashley's edition), Book V, chapter xi, para. 11, pp. 962-963. There is a fuller discussion in *Public Agency or Trading Companies, Memorials on Sanitary Reform . . . including correspondence between Mill . . . and the Metropolitan Sanitary Association* (1851), pp. 19-23. In regard to public utility policy generally, Halévy is of the opinion that " if the Radicals had come into power at the election of 1834, a consistent and well-thought-out plan might perhaps have been adopted".

justified by superior knowledge on the part of governments. They were, of course, extremely sceptical concerning the probability that the knowledge available to
governments would in fact be superior. But, conceding
the possibility, then they would argue that the release
of such knowledge would be enough. " If by chance a
Minister should become informed of any circumstance
which proved the superior advantage of a certain branch
of trade or of a certain process," said Bentham, " it
would not be a reason for employing authority in causing
its adoption. Publicity alone would produce this effect :
the more real the advantage, the more superfluous the
exercise of authority." [1]

The exceptions which they were prepared to concede
related to cases where it was thought that the ordinary
incentives were insufficient. Adam Smith was prepared
to grant a limited monopoly " when a company of
merchants undertake, at their own risk and expence, to
establish a new trade with some remote and barbarous
nation ",[2] though no one ever wrote more astringently
than he about the evils of unlimited monopolies of this
kind. J. S. Mill admitted the possible validity of the
formal argument for the protection of infant industries,[3]
though in stating this it is often omitted to explain that,
as life went on, he was shocked at the uses to which this

---

[1] Bentham, *Manual of Political Economy* : *op. cit.* vol. iii, p. 43.

[2] Adam Smith, *op. cit.* vol. ii, p. 245.

[3] Adam Smith had indeed perceived the formal argument, " By means of
such regulations [restraints on particular imports], a particular manufacture
may sometimes be acquired sooner than it could have been otherwise, and after
a certain time may be made at home as cheap or cheaper than in the foreign
country " (*op. cit.* vol. i, p. 422). But he was more sceptical than Mill. He
thought that " it will by no means follow that the sum-total, either of its
industry [*i.e.* the industry of the society] or of its revenue, can ever be augmented by any such regulation . . . the immediate effect of every such regulation is to diminish its revenue, and what diminishes its revenue is certainly not
very likely to augment its capital faster than it would have augmented of its
own accord, had both capital and industry been left to find out their natural
employments ".

argument was put and that he eventually confessed, " I am now much shaken in the opinion, which has so often been quoted for purposes which it did not warrant ; and I am disposed to think that when it is advisable, as it may sometimes be, to subsidize a new industry in its commencement, this had better be done by a direct annual grant, which is far less likely to be continued after the conditions which alone justified it have ceased to exist ".[1]

Finally, although here it may be thought that he was going rather further than some of his predecessors, Mill was prepared to concede that " in the particular circumstances of a given age or nation, there is scarcely anything really important to the general interest which it may not be desirable, or even necessary, that the government should take on itself, not because private individuals cannot effectually perform it, but because they will not. . . . This is true, more or less, of all countries inured to despotism and particularly of those in which there is a very wide distance in civilization between the people and government : as in those which have been conquered and are retained in subjection by a more energetic and more cultivated people." [2] But he goes on to add — and in this he is typical of the whole outlook of the Classical system (he was quoted with approval by Senior) [3] — that " in these cases, the mode in which the government can most surely demonstrate the sincerity with which it intends the greatest good of its subjects, is by doing the things which are made incumbent on it by the helplessness of the public, in such a manner as shall tend not to increase and per-

---

[1] *Letters of J. S. Mill* (edited Hugh Elliot), vol. ii, p. 155. See also pp. 27-28, 57-58, 116-117, 149-150.

[2] J. S. Mill, *Principles of Political Economy* (edited Ashley), Book V, chapter xi, para. 16, p. 978.

[3] *Edinburgh Review*, vol. clxxviii, October 1848, p. 331 *seq.*

petuate but to correct that helplessness. A good government will give all its aid in such a shape as to encourage and nurture any rudiments it may find of a spirit of individual exertion. It will be assiduous in removing obstacles and discouragements to voluntary enterprise . . . its pecuniary means will be applied, when practicable, in aid of private efforts rather than in supercession of them . . . government aid, when given merely in default of private enterprise, should be so given as to be as far as possible a course of education for the people in the art of accomplishing great objects by individual energy and voluntary co-operation."

(vii) *The Distribution of Property and Income*

It would be possible to multiply examples and quotations illustrating the Classical attitude to state action and the organization of production. But, with limited time at our disposal, it will be more profitable to proceed to examine a little further their attitude to problems concerning the distribution of property and income. For here we are deeper in the institutional framework and we can see even more vividly the grounds separating in their minds *agenda* from *non-agenda*.

It should be clear from what I have said already that the Classical Economists were not likely to regard the institution of property as such and the benefits flowing therefrom to the owners as in any way responsible for poverty. Property brought some sort of order into what otherwise would be chaos ; how then should its usufruct be regarded as involving a subtraction from what would otherwise be available ? " The laws, in creating property," said Bentham, " have created wealth ; but with respect to poverty, it is not the work of the laws — it is the primitive condition of the human race. The man who lives only from day to day, is precisely the man in a state of nature." [1] This follows from the arguments we have already examined. It was further thought to be powerfully reinforced by the Malthusian theory of population — of which more hereafter.

Nevertheless, as one of the sentences which I read to you from Hume will have indicated, the significance of the distribution of property as regards the sum total of happiness was not overlooked. It is quite a mistake to believe that the pseudo-law of declining social marginal utility is a recent innovation. In the *Principles of the Civil Code* and in several other places Bentham gives as unequivocal a formulation of this postulate and its consequences as anyone could wish — though, unlike some modern writers, he seems fully to have realized the essential element of arbitrariness in the calculations involved.[2] I will quote at length.

" 1. Each portion of wealth is connected with a corresponding portion of happiness.

" 2. Of two individuals, possessed of unequal fortunes, he who possesses the greatest wealth will possess the greatest happiness.

" 3. The excess of happiness on the part of the most wealthy will not be so great as the excess of his wealth.

" 4. For the same reason, the greater the disproportion between the two masses of wealth, the less the probability that there exists an equally great disproportion between the masses of happiness.

" 5. The more nearly the actual proportion approaches to equality, the greater will be the total mass of happiness." [3]

[1] Bentham, *Principles of the Civil Code*: *op. cit.* vol. i, p. 309. Compare also McCulloch, *Principles of Economics*, p. 87: " The right of property has not made poverty but it has powerfully contributed to make wealth ".
[2] See below, Lecture VI, p. 180.   [3] Bentham, *op. cit.* vol. i, p. 305.

There you have it — no mere overtone but the real thing. But it is important not to take this in isolation. Bentham is quite clear that " If all the property were to be equally divided, the certain and immediate consequence would be that there would be nothing more to divide. Everything would be speedily destroyed. Those who had hoped to be favoured by the division, would not suffer less than those at whose expense it would be made. If the condition of the industrious were not better than the condition of the idle, there would be no reason for being industrious." [1] He lays special stress upon expectation. " It is by means of this we are able to form a general plan of conduct ; it is by means of this, that the successive moments which form the duration of life are not like insulated and independent parts but become parts of a continuous whole. Expectation is a chain which unites our present and our future existence, and passes beyond us to the generations which follow. . . . The principle of security comprehends the maintenance of all these hopes ", and " Property is only a foundation of expectation ".[2] Hence " when security and equality are in opposition, there should be no hesitation : equality should give way. The first is the foundation of life — of subsistence — of abundance — of happiness ; everything depends on it : equality only produces a certain portion of happiness : besides, though it may be created, it will always be imperfect ; if it could exist for a day, the revolutions of the next day would disturb it. The establishment of equality is a chimera : the only thing which can be done is to diminish inequality." [3]

We can see views of this sort working themselves out in theories put forward with respect to inheritance and taxation.

[1] *Ibid.* p. 303.　　　[2] *Ibid.* p. 308.　　　[3] *Ibid.* p. 311.

As regards inheritance, of the three economists who seriously discussed this problem, Bentham and Mill proposed drastic innovations ; McCulloch is more conservative, though it is to be observed that, throughout, he argues each case on its merits — there is no appeal to a law of nature.

Bentham thought that the moment of death provided an opportunity of quieting the " eternal war between the two rivals, security and equality ". " Would you follow the counsels of equality without contravening those of security, wait for the natural period which puts an end to hopes and fears — the period of death." [1] He proposed limitations on the power of disposing of property by will and on the right of succession,[2] the object of a wise inheritance law being stated to be " *first*, to provide for the subsistence of the rising generation ; *secondly*, to prevent the pain of disappointment ; *thirdly*, to promote the equalization of fortunes ".

J. S. Mill went much further. As we shall see, he was sometimes not so sceptical as his predecessors concerning the eventual possibility of some forms of socialism. But it is probable that these speculations have been over-stressed and that his solid belief in property as an organizing principle has been insufficiently brought out. What is certain is that he was greatly dissatisfied with existing arrangements. " The principle of private property ", he says, " has never yet had a fair trial in any country ; and less so, perhaps, in this country than in some others. The social arrangements of modern Europe commenced from a distribution of property which was the result, not of just partition, or acquisition by industry, but of conquest and violence : and notwithstanding what industry has been doing for many centuries to modify the work of force, the system still

---

[1] Bentham, *op. cit.* vol. i, p. 312.   [2] *Ibid.* pp. 334-335.

retains many and large traces of its origin. The laws of property have never yet conformed to the principles on which the justification of private property rests. They have made property of things which never ought to be property, and absolute property where only a qualified property ought to exist. They have not held the balance fairly between human beings, but have heaped impediments upon some, to give advantage to others ; they have purposely fostered inequalities, and prevented all from starting fair in the race. That all should indeed start on perfectly equal terms is inconsistent with any law of private property : but if as much pains as has been taken to aggravate the inequality of chances arising from the natural working of the principle, had been taken to temper that inequality by every means not subversive of the principle itself ; if the tendency of legislation had been to favour the diffusion, instead of the concentration of wealth — to encourage the subdivision of the large masses, instead of striving to keep them together ; the principle of individual property would have been found to have no necessary connexion with the physical and social evils which almost all Socialist writers assume to be inseparable from it." [1] To put things right he recommended an absolute upper limit on the amount any person should be allowed to inherit — a proposal much more drastic than any which has so far been adopted in practice. I do not suggest that such a proposal would have been accepted by the earlier Classical Economists and I am not arguing that it is necessarily a sensible proposal. But it is interesting as an example of the extent to which a Classical Economist was willing to alter the framework provided he believed that the market and incentive system was not seriously affected.

Turn now to the theory of taxation and you find the

[1] J. S. Mill, *op. cit.* Book II, chapter i, para. 3.

sharpest contrast. Adam Smith, it will be remembered,
laid down the rule that the just tax was proportionate
to ability to pay — that is to say, should be roughly
proportionate to income. He was prepared to tolerate
minor deviations from this rule and even to recommend
them.[1]   But, in the main, this was his canon and this
was the Classical prescription.

Now you might expect that J. S. Mill, with his strong
disposition to loosen the scheme of possibilities wherever
prudently possible, and inheriting the Benthamite tradition of diminishing marginal social utility, would have
called this prescription in question. But, when you turn
to his chapter on the General Principles of Taxation,
you find that this is not so. He favours some exemp-
tion at the bottom of the scale but he is anxious that it
shall not be high. He then goes on to make a frontal
attack on a graduated scale.[2]

" Both in England and on the Continent a graduated
property tax (*l'impôt progressif*) has been advocated, on
the avowed ground that the state should use the instru-
ment of taxation as a means of mitigating the inequalities of wealth. I am as desirous as any one that
means should be taken to diminish those inequalities,
but not so as to relieve the prodigal at the expense of the
prudent. To tax the larger incomes at a higher percentage than the small is to lay a tax on industry and
economy; to impose a penalty on people for having
worked harder and saved more than their neighbours.
It is not the fortunes which are earned, but those which
are unearned, that it is for the public good to place under
limitation. A just and wise legislation would abstain
from holding out motives for dissipating rather than
saving the earnings of honest exertion. Its impartiality

---

[1] Adam Smith, *op. cit.* vol. ii, pp. 216 and 327.
[2] Mill, *op. cit.* p. 808.

between competitors would consist in endeavouring that they should all start fair, and not in hanging a weight upon the swift to diminish the distance between them and the slow. Many, indeed, fail with greater efforts than those with which others succeed, not from difference of merits, but difference of opportunities ; but if all were done which it would be in the power of a good government to do, by instruction and by legislation, to diminish this inequality of opportunities, the difference of fortune arising from people's own earnings could not justly give umbrage." [1]

All this, however, does not prevent him from favouring a tax on the increment of land values. And why ? The reason is clear : the incentive principle would not be violated.

[1] *Ibid.* p. 824. An interesting, if somewhat saddening, example of the current habit of using the Classical Economists as rhetorical butts, regardless of the accuracy of the allusion, is provided in Dr. Gunnar Myrdal's Ludwig Mond Lecture, reprinted in the *Manchester School*, January 1951, Vol. XIX. No. 1. Dr. Myrdal says, " We know . . . that even Mill, who tried so hard to be a free thinker, when he was faced with the concrete issue of a progressive income tax, declared that it would be worse than theft. I wonder what he would have thought if he had had a revelation of income taxes *and death duties* (my italics) in his home-land, a century hence." Who, among Dr. Myrdal's hearers, would have inferred from this that Mill had in fact put forward a plan for a form of inheritance tax much more drastic than anything which has yet come to pass and that he attached great importance to this proposal. (See the passage from Bain quoted in footnote 1, p. 151, below.)

THE CONDITION OF THE PEOPLE

(i) *Lord Lindsay on the Classical Economists*

In this lecture I want to give special attention to the
attitude of the Classical Economists to that complex of
questions which is sometimes described as the condition
of the people problem.

At this stage it is necessary first to revert to those
accusations of class interest to which I alluded in the
first lecture; for it is in connexion with the alleged
hostility of the Classical Economists to the interests of
the working classes that these accusations are most
serious. To make matters quite explicit we may take
the words of Lord Lindsay of Birker, recently Master of
Balliol; I choose Lord Lindsay, rather than others, for
critical examination, since his position in the world of
education and his repute as an expositor of the history
of philosophical thought must lend especial weight and
influence to any judgments which he feels called upon
to utter.

On page 84 of his book on *Karl Marx's Capital*, Lord
Lindsay, contrasting what he believes to be the abstract
society of individualist theory with the facts, as he
conceives them, of the real world, observes, " In the
world in which the economists [the Classical Economists,
that is to say] were actually living, some people made
profits and others were paid wages. The exchanging
was done by the people who made profits, and *it was*

in them that the economists were primarily interested "
(my italics).

On page 86, summarizing his understanding of the
Classical theory of wages, Lord Lindsay pursues the same
theme: "Thus the labour theory of value which justified
the profits of the capitalists is twisted and turned to
justify the subsistence level of wages ".

Finally, on page 94, he depicts Marxian doctrine as
" a crushing answer to the economic teaching about wages
of the early nineteenth-century economists which condemned any attempt to settle wages except by competition, which defended both the profits of the capitalists
and the subsistence wage of the wage earner ".

I am sure these quotations are fair. There is nothing
elsewhere in the book which would mitigate the force of
the indictment ; apart from a passing reference to the
scientific nature of Ricardo's interests, there is no
suspicion of a hint that the founders of economic liberalism might be conceived to have as much integrity and
compassion as the head of an Oxford College. The
Classical Economists were primarily interested in profits
and they defended subsistence wages — thus Lord Lindsay.

I will now set before you what representative Classical
Economists actually said in this connexion.

Let me begin with the founders, Adam Smith and
Malthus.

Adam Smith asks whether the contemporary improvement in the circumstances of the wage-earning classes is
an advantage or an inconvenience to society. He
answers that the answer is " abundantly plain ".
" Servants, labourers and workmen of different kinds ",
he goes on, " make up the far greater part of every great
political society. But what improves the circumstances
of the greater part can never be regarded as an incon-
veniency to the whole. No society can be flourishing and

happy, of which the far greater part of the members are poor and miserable. It is but equity, besides, that they who feed, cloath and lodge the whole body of the people, should have such a share of the produce of their own labour as to be themselves tolerably well fed, cloathed and lodged." [1]

In his *Principles*, Malthus said, " Another most desirable benefit belonging to a fertile soil is, that states so endowed are not obliged to pay much attention to that most distressing and disheartening of all cries to every man of humanity — the cry of the master manufacturers and merchants for low wages to enable them to find a market for their exports. If a country can only be rich by running a successful race for low wages, I should be disposed to say at once, perish such riches." [2]

Before the Royal Commission on Emigration, he was asked, " In a national point of view, even if it were admitted that the low rate of wages was an advantage to the capitalist, do you think it fitting that labour should be kept permanently in a state bordering on distress, to avoid the injury that might accrue to the national wealth from diminishing the rate of profit ? " This is exactly Lord Lindsay's point, and, if we followed him, we should expect an affirmative answer. In fact, the answer was as follows : " I should say by no means fitting ; I consider the labouring classes as forming the largest part of the nation, and therefore that their general condition is the most important of all." [3]

I will say nothing about Ricardo at the moment, as I intend later on to submit his views to particular examination. But it may be useful to cite McCulloch,

---

[1] Adam Smith, *op. cit.* vol. i, p. 80.

[2] Malthus, *Principles* (1st edition), p. 184. It is perhaps worth noting that Ricardo, annotating Malthus' book, made the entry " So would I " against this sentiment. *Notes on Malthus* (Hollander's edition), p. 115.

[3] Emigration Commission (1827), p. 317, Q. 3281.

who, together with James Mill, is singled out by Lord
Lindsay as particularly exemplifying the faults of the
Classical Economists.

In the index to his *Principles*, the first entry under
wages runs, " Wages, advantages of high wages, 192 ".
Turning to this reference, we find that high wages
are singled out for praise, especially in regard to the
possibility of increased leisure.

" High wages ", he says, " are advantageous only
because of the increased comforts which they bring with
them ; and of these, an addition to the time which may
be devoted to amusement is certainly not one of the
least. Wherever wages are high, and little subject to
fluctuation, labourers are found to be active, intelligent
and industrious. But they rarely prosecute their employments with the same intensity as those who are
obliged by the pressure of necessity to strain every
nerve to the utmost. They are enabled to enjoy their
intervals of ease and relaxation ; and they would be
censurable if they did not enjoy them." [1]

In the chapter on the circumstances which determine
the average rate of wages he develops the theme. " The
example of such individuals, or bodies of individuals, as
submit quietly to have their wages reduced, and who are
content if they get only mere necessaries, should never
be held up for public imitation. On the contrary, everything should be done to make such apathy be esteemed
discreditable. The best interests of society require that
the rate of wages should be elevated as high as possible —
that a taste for comforts and enjoyments should be
widely diffused and, if possible, interwoven with national
habits and prejudices. Very low wages, by rendering it
impossible for increased exertions to obtain any considerable increase of advantages, effectually hinders

---

[1] McCulloch, *Principles of Political Economy* (1843), p. 192.

them from being made, and is of all others the most powerful cause of that idleness and apathy that contents itself with what can barely continue animal existence." [1]

Clearly, a very powerful " defence of subsistence wages ".

One final example : it bears on the general attitude of the Classical Economists to labour problems in general rather than upon their attitude to the specific question of wages. I include it against the day when Lord Lindsay or some like-minded person feels called upon to write upon the wider issue. The famous Report on the Condition of the Handloom Weavers of 1841 was signed, among others, by Senior and by Overstone (S. J. Loyd, as he then was) and we know was written by Senior.[2] Discussing the effects of trade fluctuations, it expresses itself in these words : " To the higher classes of society, to those who enjoy fixed incomes . . . commercial distress is a mere name. . . . The general body of capitalists feel it but in a diminution rather of their powers of accumulation than of expenditure. But all these classes together, including those who are dependent on them, are only a minority of the population. The majority . . . are labourers, working each for his employer, and relying for his weekly subsistence solely on his weekly wages. . . . With almost all of them low wages produce immediate distress and want of employment immediate destitution. We do not believe that anyone who has not mixed with the working classes, we do not believe that we ourselves, can adequately estimate how much mental and bodily suffering, how much anxiety and pain, how much despondency and disease, are implied in the vague terms, ' a fall of

---

[1] McCulloch, *Principles of Political Economy* (1843), p. 394.

[2] Parliamentary Papers, 1841, vol. x.   An excellent appraisal of the economic content of this report is given by Professor Stigler in his *Five Lectures on Economic Problems*, pp. 26-34.

wages ', or ' a slack demand for labour.' " [1]

The fact is, I am afraid, that to accuse the Classical Economists of all people, of defending subsistence wages is to mistake the period and the school of thought. There was plenty of defence of subsistence wages in the literature of seventeenth- and eighteenth-century Mercantilism.   But it was a conspicuous feature of the Classical literature that it explicitly reversed this position.[2]

(ii) *The Theory of Population*

If we really want to understand the Classical Economists in this respect rather than denounce them or use them in rhetorical contrast to our own enlightenment, we must study the theory of population.   Indeed, to discuss their attitude to the condition of the people without discussing their view of the population problem is to play Hamlet without the Prince of Denmark.   For their beliefs in this respect were at once the basis of their fears regarding the spontaneous tendencies of the system and of their main hope of improvement through policy.

The beginning of all this, as of so much else, is to be found in the *Wealth of Nations*.   In the chapter on the " Wages of Labour " it is laid down that there is a limit " below which it seems impossible to reduce, for

[1] *Ibid.* p. 67.

[2] On the Mercantilist position see Furness, *The Position of the Labourer in a System of Nationalism*, chapter vii.   On the Classical position, the judgment of Francis Place is perhaps not without relevance.   In 1826 he wrote, for a working-men's paper, a vindication of political economy.   " The political economists ", he said, " are the great enlighteners of the people.   Look at their works from the time of the great man Adam Smith to the ' Essay on Wages ' just published by Mr. McCulloch, and see if they have not, all along, deprecated everything which was in any way calculated to do injury to the people ; see if they have not been pre-eminently the advocates for increasing the knowledge of the working classes in every possible way and then let any man say, if he can, that they have not been as pre-eminently the best friends of these classes " (*The Trades Newspaper and the Mechanics Weekly Journal*, No. 52, June 18, 1826, quoted by Wallas, *Life of Francis Place*, pp. 161-162).

any considerable time, the ordinary wages even of the lowest species of labour ". This is the rate which maintains the labourer and enables him " to bring up a family ".[1] Having regard to variations of infant mortality, Smith avoids defining closely what size family, but the inference is that it is of such a size as to maintain the population constant.

Having laid down this definition of the natural rate, he goes on to explain that there are circumstances in which rates may rise sensibly above this rate and that for long periods " When in any country the demand for those who live by wages . . . is continually increasing . . . the workmen have no occasion to combine in order to raise their wages. . . . The scarcity of hands occasions a competition among masters who bid against one another, in order to get workmen, and this voluntarily breaks through the natural combination of masters not to raise wages." [2] Such circumstances occur when " the funds which are destined for the payment of wages " are increasing. So long as capital is increasing, so long can the good time continue. Let it cease to increase, however, and the size of the working population catches up. " Though the wealth of a country should be very great, yet if it has been long stationary, we must not expect to find the wages of labour very high in it. . . . The hands, on the contrary, would . . . naturally multiply beyond their employment. . . . If in such a country the wages of labour had ever been more than sufficient to maintain the labourer, and to enable him to bring up a family, the competition of the labourers and the interests of the masters would soon reduce them to the lowest rate which is consistent with common humanity." [3] He goes on to give the dismal picture of

---

[1] Adam Smith, *op. cit.* vol. i, pp. 69-70.   [2] *Ibid.* p. 70.
[3] *Ibid.* p. 73.

eighteenth-century China, to which I referred in the first lecture.[1]

On this view, it is clear that the chief hope for the labourer is the continued increase of the funds destined for the payment of wages. Hence the strong stress on the desirability of saving.

Much the same picture of the increase of population eating into the funds destined for the payment of wages and reducing wages to subsistence level is to be found in the first edition of Malthus' *Essay on Population*. Indeed, the picture is even gloomier. For, while Adam Smith had recognized the increase in well-being of the working classes in Great Britain and had permitted himself to think of long periods of time in which the increase of the wage fund [2] sustained wages above subsistence level, the youthful Malthus, arguing against the God-winian optimism of his father and not at all averse to making the flesh creep, depicted a state of affairs in which the pressure of population on subsistence was nearly always only just round the corner ; while, in any case, the only forces by which numbers were restrained from indefinite multiplication, all resolved themselves into misery or vice.

A picture of this sort was indeed one of unrelieved gloom, and its implications for the hope of improvement utterly damping. So long as population could only be kept within the limits of subsistence by checks which involved either misery or vice, what was the use of trying ? The most careful, the most zealous efforts of reform must all be shattered on this. Let improvement be brought about, it must inevitably be transitory. Either population must automatically increase until adapted to subsistence incomes by the operation of the positive checks, war, famine, disease ; or it is prevented

---

[1] Above, p. 22 *seq.*   [2] The term, of course, comes much later.

from increasing to this point by practices — abortion, infant exposure, restrictions on freedom — which, one and all, involve vice. The picture is obviously much worse than Adam Smith's.

This, of course, is the popular idea of the typical Malthusian outlook. But, in fact, it is based on misapprehension. The picture is indeed true of the first edition of the *Essay*. But it is far from true of all subsequent editions, and it is a complete misapprehension of the views of the Classical Economists, who followed the main outlines of the Malthusian theory as stated in these editions.

Between the publication of the first and second edition of the *Essay* the views of Malthus had undergone a substantial change. Whether this was the effect of a prolonged engagement (as Cannan used to suggest in his lectures) or whether it was the effect of calmer reflection about human relations in general, by the time he came to revise his text for re-publication, Malthus had come to the conclusion that it is possible to conceive restraints upon the increase of population which were neither miserable nor vicious. " Throughout the whole of the present work ", he wrote in the Preface, " I have so far differed in principle from the former, as to suppose the action of another check to population which does not come under the heading of vice or misery ; and in the latter part I have endeavoured to soften some of the harshest conclusions of the first Essay. In doing this I hope that I have not violated the principles of just reasoning ; nor expressed any opinion respecting the probable improvement of society, in which I am not borne out by the experience of the past. To those who still think that any check to population whatever would be worse than the evils which it would relieve, the conclusions of the former essay will remain in full force :

and if we adopt this opinion we shall be compelled to acknowledge, that the poverty and misery which prevail among the lower ranks of society are absolutely irremediable." This kind of check, which involved neither misery nor vice, he called moral restraint.

It is impossible, I suggest, to exaggerate the importance of this change of emphasis in the interpretation of the Classical system. On the analytical side it meant that it was recognized that the supply price of labour was essentially a *psychological* rather than a *physiological* variable. It was the amount which would *induce* the labourer to marry and bring up children rather than the amount which would *enable* him to do so. A whole world of analytical implications springs from that.

On the side of policy, it meant even more. It meant that there was a hope that, with suitable policies, the working classes might be educated so to act as to bring it about that their numbers in relation to " funds destined to the payment of wages " were such as to afford a continually rising standard of life. The vista of a permanent emancipation from poverty opened out. Hitherto, as John Stuart Mill argued later, it was " questionable if all the mechanical inventions yet made have lightened the day's toil of any human being. They have enabled a greater population to live the same life of drudgery and imprisonment, and an increased number of manufacturers and others to make fortunes." [1] But now there was a possibility that all that might be changed. Mill himself has related in his autobiography how, among his contemporaries, when he was a young man, " Malthus's population principle was quite as much a banner, and a point of union among us, as any opinion specially belonging to Bentham. This great doctrine, originally brought forward as an argument against the indefinite

[1] J. S. Mill, *op. cit.* p. 751.

improvability of human affairs, we took up with ardent
zeal in the contrary sense as indicating the sole means of
realizing that improvability by securing full employment
at high wages to the whole labouring population through
a voluntary restriction of the increase of their numbers." [1]
And even the most austere of the Classical writers were
moved to eloquence by this prospect : " The limitation
of the number of births, by raising wages will accomplish everything that we desire, without trouble and
interference ", wrote James Mill. " The limitation
of the numbers . . . may be carried so far as . . . to raise
the condition of the labourer to any state of comfort
and enjoyment which may be desired." [2]

Ricardo developed the theme : the object should be
that the working classes should become more fastidious,
more exacting, in their demand of life. The passage
is a famous one and it might have been expected to be
well known even to the least learned of the historians of
economic and political thought. " The friends of
humanity ", he wrote, " cannot but wish that in all
countries the labouring classes should have a taste for
comforts and enjoyments, and that they should be
stimulated by all legal means in their exertions to
procure them. There cannot be a better security against
a superabundant population. In those countries where
the labouring classes have the fewest wants, and are
contented with the cheapest food, the people are exposed
to the greatest vicissitudes and miseries." [3]

And in the House of Commons he argued, " With
respect to the pressure of the taxes and the National
Debt upon the poor, that pressure could not be disputed,
especially as it took away from the rich the means

[1] J. S. Mill, *Autobiography* (World's Classics edition), pp. 88-89.
[2] James Mill, *Elements* (3rd edition), p. 67.
[3] Ricardo, *Principles* : *Works* (edited McCulloch), p. 54.

of employing the poor ; but he had no doubt if the supply of labour were reduced below the demand, which was the purpose of his Hon. and learned friend's measure, that the public debt and taxes would bear exclusively upon the rich and the poor would be most materially benefited ".[1]

Such hopes engendered most direct and practical action. We now know that it was the philosophical radicals who were responsible for the origins of the birth-control movement in this country. Malthus would not have approved of this ; for him, moral restraint meant essentially delayed marriage. He thought that wide-spread knowledge of the principle of population, coupled perhaps with a few well-chosen words from the local parson when young people came to request publication of banns, might lead to more prudent habits. But the Benthamite circle had no such inhibitions. The re-searches of Professor Field and Mr. Himes have revealed Francis Place, the friend of James Mill and Bentham, as the leading spirit in the movement to spread practical knowledge of contraceptive methods among the working classes : [2] it is believed that on one occasion the youthful John Stuart Mill was called before the police for dis-tributing birth-control literature. Certainly Mill always speaks on the subject of population with the vehemence of the social reformer. " Little improvement ", he says, " can be expected in morality until the producing of large families is regarded with the same feelings as drunkenness or any other physical excess. But while the aristocracy and clergy are foremost to set the example of this kind

---

[1] May 8, 1821, quoted by Cannan, *The Economic Outlook*, p. 121.

[2] See Field, *Essays in Population*, pp. 91-129, and Norman Himes, " The Place of John Stuart Mill and of Robert Owen in the History of English Neo-Malthusianism ", *Quarterly Journal of Economics*, 1928, vol. xlii, pp. 627-640 : also " Jeremy Bentham and the Genesis of English Neo-Malthusianism ", *Economic History III*, 1936, p. 267 *seq.*

of incontinence, what can be expected of the poor ? " [1]

It is this same belief with regard to population and wages which is responsible for the interest in profits, such as it is, which has caught Lord Lindsay's eye, in its slightly jaundiced survey of the Ricardian literature. The hope is that the workers will acquire such habits as will prevent undue multiplication and so maintain high wages. But until this happens, as Smith argued and as all the Classical Economists believed, wages can only be sustained far above subsistence level by the continued increase of the funds out of which they are paid. It would be a frustration of all hope if a stationary state should set in before habits as regards multiplication had changed. But the stationary state will set in if profits fall below the minimum which is necessary to induce accumulation. Hence corn laws and such like influences which tend to reduce profits are to be deprecated.

Again let us go to McCulloch for our demonstration; it is an odd comment on the correctness of popular mythology that, of all the Classical writers, he is perhaps the most explicit in these matters. " No country ", he writes in his section on accumulation, " can ever reach the stationary state, so long as she continues to add to

[1] Mill, *op. cit.* Book II, chapter xiii, para. 1, p. 375, footnote. For a contemporary appraisal of this attitude, see the account given in the Preface to Richard Jones' *Distribution of Wealth*, pp. xii-xiv. " But the theoretical unsoundness of these doctrines, glaring as it must be to all who are in the habit of subjecting theoretical views to the test of facts, was thrown into the shade by the fearful claims exhibited in the practical inferences to which they have been pushed . . . It was darkly, but confidently and sedulously hinted at, that the most cherished moral feelings which guide the human heart, were, after all, only a mass of superstition which it might be hoped would decay with the progress of philosophy : that means were in reserve, and ready to be circulated, of eluding the passions implanted by the creator in the original constitution of the human race ; and that at last human wisdom might be made to triumph over defects in the physical arrangements of Providence. Over the daring details with which this miserable philosophy was invested — its enduring robe of shame — and over the circumstances by which it was brought into actual contact with a part of the population, we must here draw a veil. . . ."

her capital." [1] But the average rate of profit is a test of whether this is probable. A rise of this rate " shows that the power of the society to amass capital, and to add to its wealth and population, has been increased . . . a fall . . . on the contrary is the effect of industry having become less productive and shows that the power to amass capital has been diminished, and that the progress of the society has been clogged and impeded . . . though a nation have numerous, powerful, and well-appointed armies and fleets, and the style of living among the higher classes be more than ordinarily sumptuous — still, if the rate of profit have become comparatively low, we may pretty confidently affirm that the condition of such a nation . . . is bad and unsound at bottom, that the plague of poverty is secretly creeping on the mass of her citizens ".[2]

And then in the chapter on wages : " The natural or necessary rate of wages is not therefore a fixed and un-varying quantity ; and though it be true that the market rate of wages can never sink permanently below its contemporary natural rate [note the phrase], it is no less true that the latter has a tendency to rise when the market rate rises, and to fall when it falls. The reason is, that the supply of labour can neither be speedily increased when wages rise, nor speedily diminished when they fall. When wages rise, a period of eighteen or twenty years must elapse before the effect of the in-creased stimulus given by the rise to the principle of population can be felt in the market. During all this period, therefore, the labourers have an increased command over necessaries and conveniences ; their habits are in consequence improved ; and as they learn to form more exalted notions of what is required for their comfort and decent support, the natural or

---

[1] McCulloch, *op. cit.* p. 104.   [2] *Ibid.* p. 110.

necessary rate of wages is augmented."

On the other hand : " When the rate of wages declines, either in consequence of an actual diminution of the capital appropriated to their payment, or of a disproportionate increase of population, no corresponding immediate diminution can take place in the number of labourers ".[1] " When wages are considerably reduced, the poor are obliged to economize, or to submit to live on a smaller quantity of necessaries and conveniences . . . and the danger is, that the coarse and scanty fare which has thus been in the first instance, forced on them by necessity, should in time become congenial from habit. . . . This lowering of the opinions of the labouring class with respect to the mode in which they should live, is perhaps the most serious of all the evils that can befall them." [2]

(iii) *The Ricardian Paradoxes*

It is a question which deserves examination, to what extent there was anything in the works of the Classical Economists which could afford any ground for misrepresentations of the kind we have been examining. Such misrepresentations are indeed gross ; it is difficult to think well of their authors. Nevertheless, there is enough of technicality in the Classical writings to permit sometimes of genuine misapprehension. It is, therefore, a matter of some interest to decide where misunderstandings may arise.

There can be little doubt that one of the main sources of trouble lies in the peculiar abstractions and the elliptical style of Ricardo. As we have seen already, on any level view of the facts, there can be no question of Ricardo's attitude to the interests of labour. Unless he

---

[1] McCulloch, *op. cit.* p. 392.   [2] *Ibid.* pp. 394-395.

was the most despicable hypocrite, the author of the famous passage (cited above) about the aspirations of the friends of humanity was one who wished well to the labourer. We know a good deal about the life of Ricardo and nothing that we know affords any substance for depicting him as anything else.[1] But his writings were for the most part addressed to a relatively small circle of readers whom he imagined to understand his intellectual shorthand ; and in his preoccupation with " strong cases " he often neglected to make explicit the nature of his assumptions or the limitations of his conclusions. Hot in the pursuit of new truth and oblivious of the gallery, he sometimes expressed himself in a way which was at once liable to misunderstanding and apt for misrepresentation. This happened in many connexions. In connexion with the condition of the people there are perhaps three examples which are worth attention.

First, we may note the doctrine of the tendency of wages to subsistence level. In common with the other Classical Economists, Ricardo believed that *in the absence of deliberate restraint*, the number of labourers would increase so as eventually to bring wages to subsistence level, and in his analysis of the effects of different kinds of taxes and bounties he tended to assume that this actually happened. Now there was nothing in all this of an approbatory character. Quite the contrary indeed. As we have seen, it was just this theory of how wages were determined which was the basis of his desire that the labourers might acquire expensive habits and so raise the long-run equilibrium wage above subsistence level. But, having stated his attitude on

---

[1] His attitude to the masters was perhaps more critical, as witness a letter to Trower : " Manufacturing labour is also fully employed, but the masters say they do not get their usual profits — by usual I suppose they mean unusual and exorbitant profits ". *Letters of Ricardo to Trower and Others* (edited Bonar & Hollander), p. 158.

this point, Ricardo did not go out of his way to deplore the tendencies he assumed ; and it may very well be that this may have led to misapprehension. To the unsophisticated the mere description, unaccompanied by strong expressions of dislike, of something disagreeable is often taken for approval ; and if one has had too much Hegel when one is young, the effect is sometimes not very different.

In so far as he is misunderstood or misrepresented on this score, Ricardo is surely entitled to sympathy. If one cannot have a grown-up talk about the implications of certain assumptions without it being assumed that one approves of these implications, life becomes very difficult. It is not clear, however, that he is entitled to quite so much sympathy for misunderstandings which have arisen about his propositions regarding the proportionate shares of wages and profits. Here it will be remembered that Ricardo very frequently stated that wages cannot increase save at the expense of profits and *vice versa*. Now, conceived as a statement regarding *proportionate shares*, this proposition is a truism : you cannot increase the percentage of the national dividend going as wages without diminishing the percentage going to other factors. This, of course, was Ricardo's meaning. But it was very unfortunate that he did not make this sufficiently clear and that he should often have seemed to be talking about *absolute amounts* so that, to the unwary reader, he seemed to imply that absolute wages could not increase save at the expense of profits — which he certainly did not mean and which is plainly nonsense.[1] For from such an interpretation,

---

[1] Cp. James Mill, *op. cit.* p. 75. " In this sense " (amount of commodities) " nobody has ever maintained that profits necessarily rise when wages fall, and fall when wages rise : because it was always easy to see that, by an alteration in productive power, both may rise or fall together, and also that one may rise or fall and the other remain stationary."

coupled with his declared fear of the stationary state when profits are at a minimum, for the casual or suspicious reader it was but a step to the conclusion that he favoured low wages in the absolute sense. There was no justification for such a step. There is nothing in the logic of the Ricardian system which gives any sanction to such a conclusion. We know indeed that it would have been antipathetic to his whole outlook.[1] But it must be admitted that, in this instance, his habit of using the terms of everyday speech in senses quite remote from their ordinary meaning presents a real obstacle to a proper understanding of his intentions.

The third point of doctrine where we know from experience that Ricardo is liable to misinterpretation is his discussion of taxable capacity. Here we have an example, not so much of a perverse use of words, though this is not altogether absent, as of an almost incredible unawareness of the disposition of nine-tenths of even educated humanity to read single sentences out of their context. In the chapter which is entitled *On Gross and Net Revenue* there occurs the extraordinary statement that " Provided its net real income, its rent and profits be the same, it is of no importance whether the nation consists of ten or of twelve millions of inhabitants." [2] Now, as the author himself was to protest later on, there are available in the near-by text indications which, to the careful reader, should be a sufficient clue to the author's real meaning. But if the reader is at all disposed to believe what some so-called authorities tell him about Ricardo, and if he is not alive to every

---

[1] See, *e.g.*, the striking passage in the *Notes on Malthus* (Hollander's edition). " I never wish to see the exchangeable value of the mass of commodities command more labour than usual ' at the same price ', for great as I estimate the benefits resulting from high profits I never wish to see those profits increased at the expense of the labouring class."

[2] Ricardo, *Op. cit.* pp. 210-211.

hint of implicit assumption and prepared to read the argument as a whole before drawing conclusions, he may well think that here at least he has conclusive evidence of crude capitalist bias. Provided that net revenue (profits and rents) remain the same, it does not matter whether the labouring population is large or small ; could any outlook, he may ask, be more obsessed with the interest of the property owner ?

In fact, however, such an inference would be completely false. The explanation is really very simple. The proposition occurs in the course of a discussion of taxable capacity. Now Adam Smith had argued that taxable capacity must be estimated in relation to the gross revenue — i.e. in the Classical terminology, profits, rents and wages. Ricardo, assuming that wages in the long run would be at subsistence level and arguing that, *on that assumption*, wages were not taxable, was concerned to repudiate this doctrine and relate taxable capacity, not to gross but to net revenue, i.e. profits and rents alone. This is the significance and the only significance which can properly be attached to this passage. A sufficient attention to the chapter as a whole should leave no doubt of this at all.

At this point, however, the lay reader, unlearned in the Classical system and not remembering the surrounding explanations, may be inclined to be a little sceptical. The solution, he may think, is too ingenious by half. Surely Ricardo meant what the words say, rather than this very complicated construction.

Fortunately, apart from the text itself, there is at hand evidence in favour of the explanation given, which to all candid minds must convey complete conviction. It so happens that the passage under discussion was the subject of critical comment by Say and by Malthus. They did not indeed accuse Ricardo of defending subsistence wages and depict him as a Machiavellian apologist for the propertied classes. But they did take exception to an analysis which seemed to them to regard the happiness of millions of people as a matter of indifference. Say protested that there was " une plus grande masse de bonheur " in a population of seven millions than in one of five.[1] Malthus was just as emphatic, " I can by no means agree with Mr. Ricardo in his chapter *On Gross and Net Revenue*. I should not hesitate a moment in saying that a country with a real revenue from rent and profits, consisting of food and clothing for five millions of men, would be decidedly richer and more powerful, if such real revenue were obtained from seven millions of men, rather than five, supposing them to be equally well supported. The whole produce would be greater ; and the additional two millions of labourers would some of them unquestionably have a part of their wages disposable . . . "[2]

These criticisms moved Ricardo to rejoinder. So far as Say was concerned, he was content to affix a footnote to the third edition of his *Principles* saying that Say had totally misunderstood him and appealing to the text as vindication of the claim that he was confining his remarks to Adam Smith's proposition.[3] But, in the *Notes on Malthus*, he deals at greater length with these strictures which had obviously upset him very much. First, he makes it clear that he was thinking of a case in which wages were at subsistence level, *i.e.* contained no element of net revenue, as he conceived it. " Mr. Malthus says ' The additional two millions of men would some of them unquestionably have a part of their wages disposable '. Then they would have a part of the real

---

[1] See his notes to the French translation, *Œuvres complètes de David Ricardo* (Paris, 1847), pp. 318-319.

[2] *Principles of Political Economy* (1st edition), p. 425.

[3] Ricardo, *op. cit.* p. 211.

revenue. I do not deny that wages may be such as to give to the labourers a part of the real revenue — I limited my proposition to the case when wages were too low to afford him (*sic*) any surplus beyond absolute necessaries." [1] He then reverts to the larger issue and defends himself passionately against misrepresentation. " M. Say has also remarked on this passage, and although I had carefully guarded myself, by the observation, that I was only answering Adam Smith's argument respecting the power of paying taxes, etc., and was not considering what was undoubtedly on any other occasion most worthy of consideration, the happiness of so many human beings, yet he speaks as if this consideration was wholly unimportant in my estimation. I assure him that he has done me injustice — it was not one moment absent from my mind, nor did I fail to regard it with its due weight." [2]

All this is not said by way of providing any extenuation of those critics who have made their inability to understand the basis for adverse judgment on a man so obviously their superior in moral and intellectual standing. We may condone the misapprehensions of a Say and a Malthus : they were writing at a time when a demand for further explanation was not uncalled for. But the more recent writers have not this excuse. If they took it upon themselves to deal with these matters then it was their business, if they were sincere, to make themselves aware of the present state of critical interpretation of such passages — which really leaves no room for doubt of Ricardo's meaning. It was their duty to refrain from censure before examining all the facts — to judge as they would be judged. Nothing that has been said provides any excuse whatever for their failure in

---

[1] *Notes on Malthus* (Hollander's edition), p. 207.
[2] *Ibid.* p. 208.

this respect. But it may perhaps do something to explain what has actually occurred.

(iv) *Health and Education*

With this background of general theory, we can now approach the Classical attitude to particular social problems. We may begin with health and education.

So far as health is concerned the matter is very simple. We have noted already Adam Smith's parenthesis regarding leprosy and Bentham's plan for a Ministry of Health — by which, of course, he meant a ministry responsible for sanitation and hospital services, not a Health Service on Bevan lines. There is no difference of opinion among the Classical Economists about the desirability of such services. It is perhaps worth quoting the Report on the Handloom Weavers. The Commissioners cite a very horrible return from Southwood Smith on the condition of Bethnal Green and Whitechapel and advance the opinion that " There is no ground for believing that this is a solitary or even an unusual state of things. . . . What other result can be expected, when any man who can purchase or hire a plot of ground is allowed to cover it with such buildings as he may think fit, when there is no power to enforce drainage or sewerage, or to regulate the width of streets, or to prevent houses from being packed back to back, and separated in front by mere alleys and courts, or their being filled with as many inmates as their walls can contain, or the accumulation within and without, of all the impurities which arise in a crowded population ? "

" With all our reverence for the principle of non-interference, we cannot doubt that in this matter it has been pushed too far. We believe that both the ground landlord and the speculating builder ought to be

compelled by law, though it should cost them a percentage
on their rent and profit, to take measures which shall
prevent the towns which they create being centres of
disease.   That they have not been so forced, probably
arises from the circumstance that the evils which we have
described are not felt, or even known to exist, by those
who principally influence our legislation — the higher
and middle classes. . . ." [1] Those who believe that the
Classical Economists were " primarily interested " in
profits might perhaps take note of this passage.

On education there was similar unanimity. In this
connexion Adam Smith was very explicit and very un-
conventional. He had little use for the ancient universities where he thought the fact that the teachers
were not paid by results had long ago led to their having
" given up altogether even the pretence of teaching " ;
and he certainly would have opposed state aid for such
institutions. But he thought otherwise concerning the
education of the masses. This he thought was essential
if the effects of the division of labour were not to be
disastrous for the quality of the people : and he urged
that the government should provide subsidized, but not
quite free, elementary education.

" In the progress of the division of labour ", he says,
" the employment of the far greater part of those who
live by labour, that is, of the great body of the people,
comes to be confined to a few very simple operations ;
frequently to one or two. But the understandings of the
greater part of men are necessarily formed by their
ordinary employments. The man whose whole life is
spent in performing a few simple operations, of which
the effects, too, are perhaps, always the same, or very
nearly the same, has no occasion to exert his understanding, or to exercise his invention in finding out

[1] Parliamentary Papers, 1841, vol. x, p. 73.

expedients for removing difficulties which never occur. He naturally loses, therefore, the habit of such exertion, and generally becomes as stupid and ignorant as it is possible for a human creature to become. The torpor of his mind renders him, not only incapable of relishing or bearing a part in any rational conversation, but of conceiving any generous, noble, or tender sentiment, and consequently of forming any just judgment concerning many even of the ordinary duties of private life. Of the great and extensive interests of his country he is altogether incapable of judging ; and unless very particular pains have been taken to render him otherwise, he is equally incapable of defending his country in war. The uniformity of his stationary life naturally corrupts the courage of his mind, and makes him regard with abhorrence, the irregular, uncertain, and adventurous life of a soldier. It corrupts even the activity of his body, and renders him incapable of exerting his strength with vigour and perseverance, in any other employment, than that to which he has been bred. His dexterity at his own particular trade seems, in this manner, to be acquired at the expence of his intellectual, social, and martial virtues. But in every improved and civilized society this is the state into which the labouring poor, that is, the great body of the people, must necessarily fall, unless government takes some pains to prevent it."

He therefore proposes that the public should establish " in every parish or district a little school, where children may be taught for a reward so moderate, that even a common labourer may afford it ; the master being partly but not wholly paid by the public, because if he was wholly, or even principally paid by it, he would soon learn to neglect his business . . ." like a university teacher.[1]

[1] Adam Smith, *op. cit.* vol. ii, pp. 267-268.

Malthus strongly supported this proposal, not only on the grounds put forward by Smith but also on the ground that it was desirable to make known the principle of population. " In addition to the usual subjects of instruction . . . I should be disposed to lay considerable stress on the frequent explanation of the real state of the lower classes of society, as affected by the principle of population, and their consequent dependence on themselves for the chief part of their happiness or misery." [1] He defends such reforms from the imputation that they would give rise to unrest and disorder ; the arguments are " not only illiberal but to the last degree feeble ".

I need not multiply examples. But again the Report on the Handloom Weavers affords a typical illustration of opinion some forty years later. By this time, it will be observed, compulsory education is in the picture. The Commissioners lament that " few of the labouring classes in the British Islands have received, or are receiving a good education, or have the means of obtaining one ". They urge that " The great question, whether a parent, who is by law required to provide for the bodily wants of his child, ought also to be required to attend to its mind ? has indeed, in a very limited degree, and with respect to a narrowly limited class, been decided by the Factory Act ".[2] But this is not very satisfactory. " The merit therefore of the education clauses in the Factory Act is, not what they have done, but what they have acknowledged. It is obvious at first sight, that the legislature, which fines a parent for sending a child to work at a power loom without having sent it the day before to a school, cannot consistently exempt from the same obligation the parent who sends his child to a silk mill, or to a handloom factory, or to a mine, or, in fact,

---

[1] Malthus, *Essay on Population* (edited Bettany), p. 494.
[2] Parliamentary Papers, 1841, vol. x, p. 121.

to any employment beyond his own doors. And we think that, on reflection, every one must feel that the mere accident of the child's being employed in the house of a stranger or in that of his own parent, and to go a step further, of his being or not being employed at all, does not affect the parent's obligation, or the duty of the state to enforce it. It is equally obvious that, if the state be bound to require the parent to educate his child, it is bound to see that he has the means of doing so. The voluntary system, therefore, the system which leaves to the ignorance, or negligence, or debauchery or avarice of the parents of one age to decide how far the population of the succeeding age shall, or shall not, be instructed beings, has been repudiated : and we trust that, in a matter of this importance, the most important perhaps of the many subjects requiring the attention of the Government, a system which has been repudiated on principle will not be permitted to continue in practice." [1]

After which, nothing surely remains to be said save, perhaps, that McCulloch went out of his way to include the " dexterity, skill and intelligence " of the mass of the people in his definition of national capital and to make this the pretext for a warm eulogy of the contemporary movement for popular education. [2]

(v) *The Poor Laws*

More interesting than health and education are the Poor Laws. For it is in this connexion that the Classical views regarding incentive and population give rise to an attitude which is quite different from anything which came before or after. This attitude is frequently cited.

---

[1] *Ibid.* p. 122.
[2] McCulloch, *op. cit.* pp. 117-119.

But it is seldom cited correctly, and still more seldom understood.

It is well known that Malthus and Ricardo thought the Poor Laws, as they then existed, almost wholly evil. " Their first obvious tendency ", said Malthus, " is to increase population without increasing the food for its support. A poor man may marry with little or no prospect of being able to support a family without parish assistance. They be said, therefore, to create the poor which they maintain. . . ." [1] " I feel persuaded that if the poor laws had never existed in this country, though there might have been a few more instances of very severe distress, the aggregate mass of happiness among the common people would have been much greater than it is at present." [2]

And Ricardo : " It is a truth which admits not a doubt, that the comforts and well being of the poor cannot be permanently secured without some regard on their part, or some effort on the part of the legislature, to regulate the increase of their numbers, and to render less frequent among them early and improvident marriages. The operation of the system of poor laws has been directly contrary to this. They have rendered restraint superfluous, and have invited imprudence, by offering it a portion of the wages of prudence and industry. . . . Happily these laws have been in operation during a period of progressive prosperity, when the funds for the maintenance of labour have regularly increased, and when an increase of population would be naturally called for. But if our progress should become more slow ; if we should attain the stationary state, from which I trust we are yet far distant, then will the pernicious nature of these laws become more manifest and alarming." [3]

[1] Malthus, *op. cit.* p. 342.   [2] *Ibid.* p. 344.   [3] Ricardo, *op. cit.* pp. 58-59.

For these reasons, they were in favour of total abolition, not indeed at once but by gradual stages. " Greatly as we may be shocked at such a prospect, and ardently as we may wish to remove it," wrote Malthus, " the evil is now so deeply seated, and the relief given by the poor laws so widely extended, that no man of humanity could venture to propose their immediate abolition." [1] Instead he proposed that notice should be given that no person born after a certain date (one year after the notice in the case of legitimate, two years in the case of illegitimate children) should be entitled to parish assistance. This, he thought, " would operate as a fair, distinct and precise notice " which, while not depriving of relief any living person, " would at once throw off the rising generation from that miserable and helpless dependence upon the government and the rich, the moral as well as physical consequences of which are almost incalculable ".[2]

But Malthus and Ricardo did not have the last word on this matter, so far as the Classical system was concerned. Their crude lumping together of all types of cases coming up for poor relief, though perhaps understandable in the circumstances of the time, was not likely to survive more practical examination of the problems involved. For a balanced exposition of the later Classical attitude we need to go to the works of Senior, who, though he is not to be held responsible for all the policies associated with it, is certainly to be regarded as the author of the principles of the Poor Law Amendment Act of 1834.[3]

But, to understand Senior aright, it is important to

---

[1] Malthus, *op. cit.* p. 485.　　　　[2] *Ibid.* pp. 485-486.

[3] " The report, or at least three-fourths of it, was written by me, and all that was not written by me was rewritten by me. The greater part of the Act, founded on it, was also written by me ; and in fact I am responsible for the effects, good or evil (and they must be one or the other in an enormous degree), of the whole measure." *Letters and Conversations of Alexis de Tocqueville with N. W. Senior*, 1834-59, vol. i, p. 13.

For the same reason, he favours public provision of medical treatment, the erection, regulation and support of fever hospitals, infirmaries and dispensaries. He also believes that there is a case for public provision for orphans. But he opposes special provision for old age.

There remains the case of the able-bodied and their dependants. For various reasons, when he wrote his *Letter to Lord Howick*, Senior believed it better to deal with the Irish problem by an extensive development programme rather than by creating a Poor Law where none already existed. For his mature thought on the more general problem we have to turn to the *Report of the Poor Law Commissioners* and the sundry elucidations and glosses which he gave at later dates. And there the theory is unequivocal. There is no question whatever of abolishing the right to relief. But there is the firmest insistence on the famous principle of less eligibility — the principle, namely, that the relief given must be limited to an amount which leaves the position of the relieved inferior to that of the position of the independent labourer.

The reasons for this were various. There was of course the population argument. As may be seen from their correspondence, Senior was much less impressed than Malthus with the probability that population would increase as rapidly as subsistence in most cases.[1] But there was no difference on the fundamental belief that if you made assistance an unconditional right and imposed no relative limit on its level, you encouraged improvident marriage. But beyond this, quite as much emphasis is laid upon the effects of any alternative system on the independence and character of the citizen.

---

[1] See N. W. Senior, *Two Lectures on Population, to which is added a correspondence between the author and the Rev. T. R. Malthus*. A comment on the correspondence will be found in Senior's *Political Economy* (Rosenstein-Rodan's edition), pp. 45-50.

Senior conceived the reform of the Poor Law as one of the most important stages in emancipation from feudalism. This is definitely stated in the *Edinburgh Review* article. It is perhaps even more forcibly put in the Report of the Handloom Weavers. " Under the unhappy system prevalent during the forty years immediately preceding the Poor Law Amendment Act, a large portion of the labourers of England were treated not as freemen but as slaves or domestic animals, and received not strictly speaking wages, regulated by the value of their labour, but rations proportioned to their supposed wants. . . . Under such circumstances, wages, if we can apply the term to payments so regulated, rose and fell with the price of bread, just as the keep of a horse rises or falls with the price of oats."

It is no part of my business here to linger on the details of this matter — on the difference between the workhouse which Senior recommended and the workhouse which actually came into being. On all these matters I refer you to the admirable account by Dr. Marian Bowley.[1] I must not, however, refrain from quoting John Stuart Mill, lest in the absence of some reference to him, you might think that there was some detachment on his part from a point of view which was certainly fully endorsed by other contemporary Classical Economists and which there is reason to believe was approved in the last years of his life by Malthus.

Mill says, " The famous Act of the 43rd of Elizabeth undertook, on the part of the public, to provide work and wages for all the destitute able-bodied : and there is little doubt that if the intent of that Act had been fully carried out, and no means had been adopted by the

---

[1] M. Bowley, *Nassau Senior and Classical Economics*. It is one of the regrettable results of the interruption of scholarly study during the last ten years that this excellent work has not yet received the attention it deserves.

realize that the Report of the Poor Law Commissioners, with which he had so much to do, quite explicitly confines itself to the problem of the able-bodied applicants for relief. For a comprehensive view of his general position we have to go further afield and take into account his *Letter to Lord Howick*, his article on the " English Poor Laws " in the *Edinburgh Review*,[1] and various *obiter dicta* scattered up and down elsewhere.

According to the *Letter to Lord Howick*, the great test which must be applied to any project of state action in regard to relief is the question *whether it has any tendency to increase that which it is proposed to relieve*. This is very important ; it makes explicit the dominating principle underlying the general Classical attitude. " As far as the poor are concerned," he says, " to make the supply of relief adequate to the demand for it ; and, as far as the rich are concerned, to apportion equally the burthen of affording that relief . . . these are noble purposes, and as far as they can be effected without materially diminishing industry, forethought and charity, it is the imperious duty of Government to effect them."

Thus he is all in favour of provision for the blind, the insane, the chronic invalid and the maimed. " No public fund for the relief of these calamities has any tendency to diminish industry or providence. They are evils too great to allow individuals to make any sufficient provision against them, and too rare to be, in fact, provided against by them at all. Their permanency, too, is likely to weary out private sympathy. And the worst of them, madness, is perhaps the calamity with which we least adequately sympathize. Even to educated persons the insane are too frequently objects of aversion. I wish, therefore, to see these evils met by an ample compulsory provision." [2]

[1] October 1841.   [2] Senior, *op. cit.* p. 14.

administrators of relief to neutralize its natural tendencies, the poor-rate would by this time have absorbed
the whole net produce of the land and labour of the
country. It is not at all surprising, therefore, that Mr.
Malthus and others should at first have concluded
against all poor laws whatever. It required much experience, and careful examination of different modes of
poor-law management, to give assurance that the admission of an absolute right to be supported at the cost of
other people, could exist in law and in fact, without
fatally relaxing the springs of industry and the restraints
of prudence. This, however, was fully substantiated by
the investigations of the original Poor Law Commissioners. Hostile as they are unjustly accused of
being to the principle of legal relief, they are the first
who fully proved the compatibility of any Poor Law,
in which a right to relief was recognized, with the
permanent interests of the labouring class and of
posterity. By a collection of facts, experimentally
ascertained in parishes scattered throughout England,
it was shown that the guarantee of support could be
freed from its injurious effects upon the minds and habits
of the people, if the relief, though ample in respect to
necessaries, was accompanied with conditions which they
disliked, consisting of some restraints on their freedom,
and the privation of some indulgences. Under this
proviso, it may be regarded as irrevocably established,
that the fate of no member of the community needs be
abandoned to chance; that society can and therefore
ought to insure every individual belonging to it against
the extreme of want; that the condition even of those
who are unable to find their own support, needs not be
one of physical suffering, or the dread of it, but only of
restricted indulgence, and enforced rigidity of discipline. This is surely something gained for humanity,

important in itself, and still more so as a step to something beyond ; and humanity has no worse enemies than those who lend themselves, either knowingly or unintentionally, to bring odium on this law, or on the principles in which it originated." [1]

(vi) *Contract and Factory Legislation*

It is now time to move closer to the actual activities of the wage earners and to inquire concerning the attitude of the Classical Economists to the questions which arise in this connexion. We may begin with the form of the labour contract and the conditions it is allowed to assume. After that we may proceed to the actual settlement of wages and the role of combinations.

So far as the form of the labour contract was concerned, it is perhaps worthy of remark that, with one exception, the Classical Economists were opposed to truck payments. Adam Smith has the argument : " The law which obliges the masters in several different trades to pay their workmen in money and not in goods, is quite just and equitable. It imposes no real hardship on the masters. It only obliges them to pay that value in money which they pretended to pay, but did not always really pay, in goods." [2] The exception was Ricardo — not because he had a private truck shop himself; so far as I know he had not — but because Robert Owen's experiments would be impeded by prohibition. " Mr. Owen prided himself upon having introduced the provision system. He had opened a shop at New Lanark in which he sold the best com-

---

[1] Mill, *op. cit.* Book II, chapter xii, para. 3, pp. 365-366.
[2] Adam Smith, *op. cit.* vol. i, p. 143 ; Cannan, *The Economic Outlook, Ricardo in Parliament*, p. 117.

modities to his workmen cheaper than they could be obtained elsewhere ; and he was persuaded that the practice was a beneficial one."

As regards the Factory Acts proper, Smith does not mention them since they did not arise in his time ; and we do not know Ricardo's attitude. There is, however, plenty of evidence that the other Classical Econo- mists approved of restrictions on the employment of children. Malthus goes out of his way to approve Robert Owen's agitation. " Mr. Owen is, I believe, a man of real benevolence, who has done much good ; and every friend of humanity must heartily wish him success in his endeavours to procure an Act of Parlia- ment for limiting the hours of working among the children in the cotton manufactories, and preventing them from being employed at too early an age." [1] Francis Horner, in a speech on the Bill of 1815, said that the former measure and even the present Bill, so far as he could understand its object, fell far short of what Parliament should do on this subject.[2] Senior, who on account of his *Letters on the Factory Acts* is commonly regarded as an utter reactionary in this respect, says in the preface to the selfsame letters, " No facts have been proved to me, and I do not believe that any exist, which show that it is proper to keep a child of eleven years old, for twelve hours a day, in attendance on the employment, however light, of a factory ".[3] Finally, in 1833, McCulloch wrote to Lord Shaftesbury in the following terms : " I hope your Factory Bill will prosper and I am glad it is in such good hands. Had I a seat

---

[1] Malthus, *op. cit.* p. 319.

[2] *Memoirs and Correspondence of Francis Horner* (edited Leonard Horner), vol. ii, p. 256.

[3] Senior, *Letters on the Factory Act,* etc. (1st edition), p. 9. On the episode of Senior's *Letters* and the use made of them by some subsequent historians, see M. Bowley, *op. cit.* pp. 255-258, especially the footnote on p. 257.

in the House it should assuredly have my vote. A notion is entertained that political economists are, in all cases, enemies to all sorts of interference, but I assure you I am not one of those who entertain such an opinion. I would not interfere between adults and masters ; but it is absurd to contend that children have the power to judge for themselves as to such a matter . . . if your Bill has any defect, it is not by the too great limitation, but by the too great extension of the hours of labour." [1]

The great problem related to the position of women. There was general agreement that interference as regards hours was undesirable where adult males were concerned — although J. S. Mill developed a hypothetical argument in its favour expressly stated to have no contemporary significance.[2] But the status of women in this respect was in doubt. In general, it was thought to be wrong that they should not be treated as being as responsible as men. Senior conceded an exception to this in regard to female labour in mines, though he thought that the unfortunate women who were thus prevented from working should have been regarded as eligible for compensation.[3] Apart from this, he thought such legislation harmful. Mill was a little more guarded, but thought that the classing together of women and children was " indefensible in principle and mischievous in practice ". " Women are as capable as men ", he said, " of appreciating and managing their own concerns, and the only hindrance to their doing so arises from the injustice of their present social position. . . . If women had as absolute a control as men have over their own persons and their own patrimony or acquisitions, there

---

[1] Hodder, *Life of Shaftesbury*, vol. i, pp. 157-158. The letter is quoted by Dicey in his *Law and Opinion on England*.

[2] Mill, *op. cit.* Book V, chapter xi, para. 11, pp. 963-964.

[3] *Oxford Lectures, 1847–48.* (Unpublished, but reproduced in part in Levy, *op. cit.* vol. ii, pp. 308-311.)

would be no plea for limiting their hours of labouring for themselves in order that they might have time to labour for the husband, in what is called, by the advocates of restriction, *his* home. Women employed in factories are the only women in the labouring ranks of society whose position is not that of slaves and drudges ; precisely because they cannot easily be compelled to work and earn wages in factories against their will. For improving the position of women, it should on the contrary be an object to give them the readiest access to independent industrial employment, instead of closing, entirely or partially, that which is already open to them." [1]

(vii) *Wages and Combinations*

Finally, we may take a brief glance at the Classical attitude to the various influences actually determining the heart of the wage contract — the rate of wages itself.

It is a natural application of the general theory of the market that wage rates in particular lines of industry depend fundamentally upon the influences underlying supply and demand. This was the view of the Classical Economists. Assuming the absence of obstacles to mobility, they thought that there would be profound influences tending to keep rates in different occupations in close relation with one another. But this did not prevent them seeing that, in the absence of mobility, changes in the conditions of demand and supply might bring about divergencies which might be very painful : the plight of the handloom weavers was a dreadful example of this.

It is safe to say, however, that it would never have occurred to them to arrest change in the interests of particular groups. Bentham indeed in the *Manual of*

---

[1] Mill, *op. cit.* Book V, chapter xi, para. 9, p. 959.

Political Economy says that " opposition to machinery
is well-grounded, if no care be taken to provide immediate employment for the discharged hands ".[1]   And
Torrens, in his *Wages and Combinations*, was so moved by
the position of the handloom weavers that he urged the
formation of a compensation fund for their relief and,
somewhat on the lines since developed by Professor
Hutt, urged that " whenever a new application of
mechanical power throws a particular class of operatives
out of employment, a national fund should be provided,
to aid them in betaking themselves to other occupations ".[2]   But the idea that change should be stopped
would have been utterly antipathetic — reminiscent of
the errors of the mercantile system and sacrificing general
advancement to sectional interest.   No, they would
argue, when everything has been done to create new
outlets by the general policy of freeing international
trade, the correct policy in such cases is to do all that
is possible to foster mobility — remove monopoly elsewhere and provide an education which makes it easier
for the workmen to learn new jobs.   The Report on the
Handloom Weavers is a classic example of the application of these principles.

It goes almost without saying that men in this frame
of mind were opposed to wage-fixing by authority —
either maximum or minimum.   This is very clearly laid
down by Bentham in the *Manual*.   " The fixation of the
rate of wages in order to prevent their excess ", he says,
" is a favour conferred on the rich at the expense of the
poor — on the master at the expense of the workman.
It is a violation, with regard to the weakest class, of the
principles of security and property."   On the other hand,
" to fix the minimum of wages, is to exclude from labour

---

[1] Bentham, *op. cit.* vol. iii, p. 39 ; see also pp. 67-68.
[2] Torrens, *Wages and Combinations* (1834), p. 44.

many workmen who otherwise would have been employed ; it is to aggravate the distress you wish to relieve. In fact, all that can be done is limited to determining, that if they are employed, they shall not receive less than the price fixed : it is useless to enact that they shall be employed. Where is the farmer, where is the manufacturer, who will submit to employ labourers who cost them more than they yield ? " [1]

On the same grounds, the authors of the Report on the Handloom Weavers reject the proposal for tribunals to raise the weavers' wages or to prevent their fall. " It is obvious that laws for such a purpose . . . must have a tendency by raising the price of the weavers' labour to diminish the demand for it, while, by holding out the expectation of a higher reward, they would increase the supply." [2]

But what about voluntary combinations of labourers to fix wages ? What was the attitude of the Classical Economists to trade unions ?

Now it must be realized that the whole spirit of the Classical outlook was opposed to monopoly. As Professor Hecksher remarks, the Classical Economists sympathized with the state and with the individual citizens but not with intermediate bodies claiming coercive power.[3] Their sympathies with the worker, which were real, were contingent upon his service to the consumer. There was nothing in their system to justify any predisposition in favour of groups of producers exercising restriction vis-à-vis the rest of the community.

It follows therefore that, from the outset, there must have been much in the outlook and spirit of trade unionism which was necessarily antipathetic to the

[1] Bentham, op. cit. vol iii, p. 66.
[2] Parliamentary Papers, 1841, vol. x, p. 49.
[3] Hecksher, Mercantilism, vol. ii, p. 329.

Classical Economists. This comes out very forcibly in the final section of Mill's famous chapter *On the Probable Future of the Labouring Classes*. There he argues that while he agrees with socialists in desiring a transformation of productive organization in the direction of co-operation, he " utterly " dissents " from the most conspicuous and vehement part of their teaching, their declamations against competition. With moral conceptions in many respects far ahead of the existing arrangements of society, they have in general very confused and erroneous notions of its actual working ; and one of their greatest errors, as I conceive, is to charge upon competition all the economical evils which at present exist. They forget that wherever competition is not, monopoly is ; and that monopoly, in all its forms, is the taxation of the industrious for the support of indolence, if not of plunder. They forget, too, that with the exception of competition among labourers, all other competition is for the benefit of the labourers, by cheapening the articles they consume ; that competition even in the labour market is a source not of low but of high wages, wherever the competition *for* labour exceeds the competition *of* labour, as in America, in the colonies, and in the skilled trades ; and never could be a cause of low wages, save by the overstocking of the labour market through the too great numbers of the labourers' families." [1] " Instead of looking upon competition as the baneful and anti-social principle which it is held to be by the generality of Socialists, I conceive that, even in the present state of society and industry, every restriction of it is an evil and every extension of it, even if for a time injuriously affecting some class of labourers, is always an ultimate good." [2]

Nevertheless, a belief in liberty of association was a

[1] Mill, *op. cit.* Book IV, chapter vii, para. 7, p. 792.   [2] *Ibid.* p. 793.

very strong feature of the Classical outlook; and the fact must be recognized that, once the war with Napoleon had been brought to an end, there were none more forward than the Classical Economists and their friends to agitate for the repeal of the laws that prohibited the combination of wage earners; the story of how Francis Place and Joseph Hume carried out this propaganda is well known.[1] Now Francis Place was an intimate friend of James Mill and Jeremy Bentham; and the attitude of the Classical Economists to what he was doing is well set out in McCulloch's *Essay on the Circumstances which Determine the Rate of Wages and the Condition of the Labouring Classes*, which was published in 1826. McCulloch's main case rests upon the injustice, as he sees it, of preventing combination. " Capacity to labour is to the poor man what stock is to the capitalist. But you would not prevent a hundred or a thousand capitalists from forming themselves into a company, or *combination* who should take all their measures in common, and dispose of their property as they might, in their collective capacity, judge most advantageous for their interests :— and why then should not a hundred or a thousand labourers be allowed to do the same by *their stock* ? " [2] He is quite clear that the competition of masters may be trusted in the long run to raise wages that have been unduly depressed; and he does " not believe that the combination laws had the slightest effect on the average and usual rate of wages ". But that is no reason why workmen should be prevented from combining. Moreover, combination may bring about a more immediate rise to the normal level; where it is prevented " more or less time must always elapse before the high profits

---

[1] Graham Wallas, *The Life of Francis Place*, chapter viii.
[2] McCulloch, *op. cit.* p. 185. See also a letter from Ricardo to McCulloch on the same subject, *Letters of Ricardo to McCulloch* (edited Hollander), p. 87.

caused by the undue reduction of wages becomes generally known and consequently before capital can be attracted from other businesses ".[1] He ridicules fears of monopoly : it must be almost as difficult to form as a monopoly of bread,[2] and if it were formed it would speedily break down, therefore a " combination for an improper object, or to raise wages above their proper level, must *cure itself* ".[3] He laments the outbreak of strikes and disorder which had followed repeal and makes it quite plain that he is utterly against the use of violence on the part of the workmen. But he argues that it is still early to judge the outcome. The workmen have thought themselves oppressed for so long that some abuses in the use of their new liberty are not surprising. Given time, it is to be hoped that they would learn greater wisdom. Place went even further and thought that when the Combination Laws were repealed workmen's combination would disappear.[4]

But the combinations did not disappear, and as time went on there became apparent in the Classical literature, particularly in the work of Senior and J. S. Mill, new heart-searching concerning their scope and significance. Senior was very apprehensive of the unions. It is said that in 1830 he made very strong recommendations to Lord Melbourne for limiting their powers ;[5] certainly, in the Report on the Handloom Weavers, the section on combinations develops a formidable indictment of the unionism of the day, in regard both to its resort to

---

[1] McCulloch, *op. cit.* p. 188.   [2] *Ibid.* pp. 189-190.
[3] *Ibid.* p. 192.   [4] Wallas, *op. cit.* p. 217.
[5] See the *History of Trade Unionism* (1920 edition), by S. and B. Webb, pp. 139-141. The document on which this account is based was not available when Dr. Bowley searched for it ; and until it turns up again I am inclined to think that it is better to rely on the extract which was included in the Report on the Handloom Weavers and reproduced with a prefatory note by Senior in his *Historical and Philosophical Essays* (1865), prepared for publication in 1862 shortly before his death.

bodily violence and to the damage and injustice which he thought it did to unskilled workers by excluding them from occupations in which they could speedily learn to be useful. He argued against a return to the old combination laws. But he was in favour of a strengthening of the law to prevent combinations forcing discharges of individual labourers and the use or prohibition of certain sorts of machinery; and he believed that picketing should be made a criminal offence.[1]

J. S. Mill, on the other hand, was much more favourable to the unions. Both in his *Principles* and in his famous review of *Thornton on Labour and its Claims*,[2] he extends himself to provide every justification he can think of for their actions, even going so far as to outline a possible Malthusian argument for the sectional monopoly of the skilled, namely, that, so long as the unskilled continue to multiply blindly, " preventing them from competing does them no real injury " : it only prevents everyone being brought down to the same level. But even in Mill we find profound hesitations concerning the way in which the power of the unions was often used. " There must be some better mode of sharing the fruits of human productive power than by diminishing their amount. Yet this is not only the effect but the intention of many of the conditions imposed by some Unions on workmen and on employers. All restrictions on the employment of machinery, or on arrangements for economising labour, deserve this censure. Some of the union regulations go even further than to prohibit improvements; they are contrived for the express purpose of making work inefficient; they positively prevent the workmen from working hard and well . . ."[3] and more to the same effect.

---

[1] Mill *op. cit.* p. 116.

[2] Reprinted in *Dissertations and Discussions*, vol. iv, pp. 25-85.

[3] *Ibid.* pp. 80-81.

Thus a profound unease and uncertainty dominates the work of the later Classical Economists when they are confronted with the problem of workers' combinations.[1]

[1] I have made no allusion in the above discussion to the Classical theory of the Wage Fund. This for the very simple reason that, contrary to popular belief, the Wage Fund theory was not used by the Classical Economists as an argument against working-class pressure for higher wages. The whole matter has been exhaustively examined by Taussig in his *Wages and Capital*, especially chapter x. Taussig concludes : " The sting of the doctrine, as it was attacked and reprobated in later days, was in the supposed predetermination and rigidity of the wages fund : in the obstacles which it was supposed to present against efforts at immediate improvement in the condition of labourers. Whatever may have been the case in later years, there is no evidence that fixity or rigidity in the wage fund was prominent in the minds of the writers of the period considered in the present chapter (' From Ricardo to John Stuart Mill '). Such evidence as we get on this point, derived mainly from their discussion of combinations and strikes, is in the negative. The wages fund is there certainly not described as rigid, and by inference is treated as elastic."

THE CLASSICAL ECONOMISTS AND SOCIALISM: HUME TO SENIOR

(i) *Introduction*

HAVING come thus far, it seems natural to push the inquiry a little further and to ask what was the attitude of the Classical Economists to other proposals for change in the future organization of society. What was their attitude, if any, to the fundamental socialist ideas of public ownership and operation of the means of production and a distribution of income not influenced by the operations of the market ?

To this question the short answer must be that materials for a full answer are lacking. Socialists have seldom been very explicit in their plans for the future organization of society ; and at the time at which the Classical Economists, as here defined, were writing these plans were even less well defined than they have been since. At the beginning of the period, indeed, it would be difficult to point to a body of what could reasonably be called specifically socialist thought ; from the time of Plato onwards there had been projects of ideal commonwealths, there had been recurrent waves of levelling sentiment ; but of socialist analyses and socialist programmes, in the sense in which we now understand the words, there was hardly anything but fragmentary anticipation. Later on things began to change. But it was not until the later part of our period that there began to appear a body of argument and suggestions which, from the point of view of the Classical Economists, would seem to call for extensive comment. Nevertheless, although it is only in the work of John Stuart Mill that we find any serious and systematic consideration of this sort of thing, yet scattered about the works of the earlier writers we find allusions and *obiter dicta* which are perhaps worth gathering together. It would be surprising if the literature of one of the main branches of individualism threw no oblique light on the attitude of its authors to the opposing point of view ; and the case of John Stuart Mill certainly deserves quite extensive study. In this lecture, therefore, I shall try to piece together the various fragments on this subject which are to be found in the works of the English Classical writers from Hume to Senior, reserving for the next lecture a more thorough examination of the more systematic work of John Stuart Mill. In both these lectures, since my subject matter is less well known than what I have had to deal with hitherto, my treatment, although making no claim to be exhaustive, will be more detailed than it has been so far. It will, moreover, make more distinction between the works of different authors and, where John Stuart Mill is concerned, between the different works of the same author.

(ii) *Hume and Adam Smith*

There is no systematic discussion of collectivism in the works of Hume or Adam Smith. Nevertheless, it is not at all difficult to infer indirect latent attitudes.

As we have seen already, Hume's theory of property is essentially based on considerations of utility. You can conceive circumstances in which the institution of property would be unnecessary or in which it would have to be superseded : in a state of abundance it is not called for ; in a state of siege it breaks down ; a state of universal benevolence would render it superfluous. But in normal circumstances, where the means of satisfaction are scarce, but not so intensely scarce as in a siege, and where self-love and family affection are so much stronger than general altruism, it seems the most workable basis for order in social life. Hume understands quite well that there are circumstances in which governmental action is necessary to supplement the actions which spring from the ownership of property : there is a passage in the *Treatise* which sets out as well as could possibly be desired the nature of the circumstances in which an abdication of certain rights of individual action may be in the interest of all individuals.[1] But he takes it for granted that private property must be the main basis for social co-operation ; and although he does not explicitly discuss common ownership in this connexion, it is reasonable to infer that the emphasis

---

[1] Hume, *A Treatise of Human Nature* (edited Green and Grose), vol. ii, p. 304. " Two neighbours may agree to drain a meadow, which they possess in common : because it is easy for them to know each other's mind ; and each must perceive, that the immediate consequence of his failing in his part, is the abandoning the whole project. But it is very difficult, and indeed impossible, that a thousand persons should agree in any such action ; it being difficult for them to concert so complicated a design, and still more difficult for them to execute it ; while each seeks a pretext to free himself of the trouble and expense, and would lay the whole burden on others. Political society easily remedies both these inconveniences. Magistrates find an immediate interest in the interest of any considerable part of their subjects. They need consult nobody but themselves to form any scheme for the promoting of that interest. And as the failure of any one piece in the execution is connected, though not immediately, with the failure of the whole, they prevent that failure, because they find no interest in it, either immediate or remote. Thus, bridges are built, harbours opened, ramparts raised, canals formed, fleets equipped, and armies disciplined, everywhere, by the care of government, which, though composed of men subject to all human infirmities, becomes, by one of the finest and most subtile inventions imaginable, a composition which is in some measure exempted from all these infirmities."

on the necessity for private ownership implies a deliberate rejection of the alternative.

This conclusion is conjectural. But a passage in the essay *Of Commerce*, in which Hume depicts the difficulties of military socialism considered as a permanent institution, is very strong supporting evidence. " Could we convert a city into a kind of fortified camp," he says, " and infuse into each breast so martial a genius, and such a passion for public good, as to make everyone willing to undergo the greatest hardships for the sake of the public, these affections might now, as in ancient times, prove alone a sufficient spur to industry, and support the community. It would then be advantageous, as in camps, to banish all arts and luxury ; and by restrictions on equipage and tables, make the provisions and forage last longer than if the army were loaded with a number of superfluous retainers. But as these principles are too disinterested, and too difficult to support, it is requisite to govern men by other passions and animate them with a spirit of avarice and industry, art and luxury. The camp is, in this case, loaded with a superfluous retinue ; but the provisions flow in proportionably larger. The harmony of the whole is still supported ; and the natural bent of the mind, being more complied with, individuals, as well as the public, find their account in the observance of these maxims." [1]

As regards principles of distribution other than those implied by the institution of property and inheritance, as we have already seen he goes out of his way to acknowledge the strong *prima facie* case for equal distribution.[2] But, as we have also seen, he is emphatic in his rejection of this principle. It will not work, and the attempt to make it work must lead to impoverishment

---

[1] *Essays, Moral, Political and Literary* (edited Green and Grose), vol. i, pp. 294-295.   [2] Lecture II above, p. 52.

and loss of freedom.[1] It should be noted, however, that in this connexion he was thinking, not of a system of equal incomes based on common ownership, but rather of attempts to bring about a persistent equality in the distribution of property. The Levellers to whom he refers were distributivist radicals ; there was nothing specifically communistic about their proposals.

Explicit references to collectivism, in the modern sense of the term, are even harder to find in Adam Smith than in Hume. There is, of course, his allusion to Utopia and Oceana as representing limiting cases of improbable developments. But the reference here is to the improbability of ideal commonwealths of any kind, rather than to the specific undesirability of any collectivist tendencies in the work of More or Harrington. Smith was too much preoccupied in developing his own analysis and the system of policy which flowed from it, to be turned aside into discussion of anything which would have seemed to him to be so inherently fantastical as nineteenth-century collectivism.

Nevertheless, in an indirect way, the critique of the mercantile system to which so much of this book was devoted may be legitimately construed as implying an attitude on this problem. The case against Mercantilism, as Smith saw it, seems to rest on a twofold basis : on the one hand, it fostered privilege ; on the

---

[1] This is not to say that Hume was indifferent to the degree of inequality prevailing. On the contrary, in his essay *Of Commerce* he drew attention to the desirability of the multiplicity of mechanic arts as tending to the diminution of inequality. " A too great disproportion among the citizens weakens any state. Every person, if possible, ought to enjoy the fruits of his labour, in a full possession of all the necessaries, and many of the conveniences of life. No one can doubt, but that such an equality is most suitable to human nature, and diminishes much less from the *happiness* of the rich than it adds to that of the poor. . . . Add to this, that, where the riches are in few hands these must enjoy all the power, and will readily conspire to lay the whole burthen [of taxes] on the poor, and oppress them still further to the discouragement of all industry."

other, it involved a misdirection of resources. Now it is perhaps an argument against collectivism, that, as it works out in practice, it tends to consolidate privilege ; it is possible to imagine a case on these lines being built upon experience since then. But it would be absurd to attribute such an argument to Adam Smith — the positions of privilege which may be fostered by modern collectivism are not the same as the positions he was attacking. It is not so absurd, however, to imagine him applying to a hypothetical collectivism the arguments which he directed against Mercantilism on the score of misdirection of resources. For it was certainly one of his main contentions that central authority was incompetent to decide on a proper distribution of resources. I have quoted already the famous remark about the statesman " who should attempt to direct private people in what manner they ought to employ their capitals ". You remember that such a man is depicted as assuming " an authority which could safely be trusted, not only to no single person, but to no council or senate whatever, and which would nowhere be so dangerous as in the hands of a man who had folly and presumption enough to fancy himself fit to exercise it ".[1] That seems to indicate a pretty deep-rooted distrust of central direction of the organization of production. This is reinforced by the statement later on, when he is describing the duties of the sovereign, that he is entirely discharged from the duty of " superintending the industry of private people, and of directing it towards the employments most suitable to the interest of the society — a duty ", says Smith, " in the attempting to perform which he must always be exposed to innumerable delusions, and for the proper performance of which no human wisdom or knowledge could ever be

[1] Lecture I above, p. 18.

sufficient ".[1] Whether this be right or wrong, it has certainly remained one of the chief arguments against total collectivism from then until the present day.

The same point is made, perhaps even more forcibly, in the famous passage in the *Theory of Moral Sentiments* on the man of system : " The man of system . . . is apt to be very wise in his own conceit ; and is often so enamoured with the supposed beauty of his own ideal plan of government, that he cannot suffer the smallest deviation from any part of it. He goes on to establish it completely and in all its parts, without any regard either to the great interests, or to the strong prejudices which may oppose it. He seems to imagine that he can arrange the different members of a great society with as much ease as the hand arranges the different pieces upon a chess-board. He does not consider that the pieces upon the chess-board have no other principle of motion besides that which the hand impresses upon them ; but that, in the great chess-board of human society, every single piece has a principle of motion of its own, altogether different from that which the legislature might choose to impress upon it. If those two principles coincide and act in the same direction, the game of human society will go on easily and harmoniously, and is very likely to be happy and successful. If they are opposite or different, the game will go on miserably, and the society must be at all times in the highest degree of disorder." [2]

(iii) *Bentham*

When we turn to Bentham, the third great founder of the Classical theory of policy, we find a much more

[1] Adam Smith *op. cit.* vol. ii, p. 184.

[2] 6th edition, vol. ii, pp. 110-111. My attention was drawn to the relevance of this passage by Professor H. M. Robertson's recent lecture on " European

explicit treatment of these issues. The amount of space devoted to them is indeed small. But there is no doubt of the significance of what is actually said. Both in regard to what he called the Levelling System and in regard to the community of goods, Bentham had a coherent position.

Let us begin with his attitude to the Levelling System. Bentham was by no means oblivious of the strength of the case which can be made for diminishing inequality ; and, as we have seen, he made specific proposals for attaining this end. But he had no use for systems of equality as such and he regarded proposals for the abolition of property with a view to maintaining equality as fraught with disaster.

" If violent causes, such as a revolution in government, a schism, a conquest, produce the overthrow of property," he says, " it is a great calamity ; but it is only transitory — it may be softened and even repaired by time. Industry is a vigorous plant, which resists numerous loppings, and in which the fruitful sap rises immediately upon the return of spring. But if property were overthrown with the direct intention of establishing equality of fortune, the evil would be irreparable : no more security — no more industry — no more abundance ; society would relapse into the savage state from which it has arisen,

Devant eux des cités, derrière eux des déserts." [1]

He thinks that a state of equality can only be preserved " by the same violence by which it was established. It would require an army of inquisitors and executioners. . . . The level must be in perpetual motion in order to smooth down whatever would rise above the legal line.

Economic Development in the Sixteenth Century ", *South African Journal of Economics*, vol. xviii, p. 36.
    [1] Bentham, *Principles of the Civil Code* : *op. cit.* vol. i, pp. 311-312.

Watchfulness must be uninterrupted, to restore the lack of those who have dissipated their portion, and to strip those who by means of labour have augmented, or by care have preserved, theirs. In such a state of things prodigality would be wisdom and none but the mad would be industrious. . . ."

His attitude to proposals for the community of goods is no less outspoken.

" There is no arrangement more contrary to the principle of utility ", he says, " than community of goods, especially that kind of indeterminate community in which the whole belongs to everyone." He argues that it is a source of discord, of waste and of concealed inequality. He goes out of his way to exempt what he calls servitudes — rights of way, rights of water, but he praises the enclosure of common land, where " harvests, flocks and smiling habitations, have succeeded to the sadness and sterility of the desert ".[1]

Elsewhere he contemplates the mechanics of societies founded on this principle :

" Some small societies, in the first effervescence of religious enthusiasm, have instituted, as a fundamental principle, the community of goods. Has happiness been increased thereby ? The gentle motive of reward has been supplied [supplanted ?] by the doleful motive of punishment. Labour so easy and light when animated by hope, has been represented as a penance necessary to escape from eternal punishments. Hence, so long as the religious motive preserves its force, everyone labours, but everyone groans. Does this motive grow weaker ? The society divides itself into two classes : the one, degraded fanatics, contract all the vices of an unhappy superstition ; the other, idle cheats, cause themselves to be supported in their idleness by the dupes by whom

[1] *Ibid.* pp. 341-342.

they surround themselves ; whilst the cry for equality is only a pretext to cover the robbery which idleness perpetrates upon industry."

Thus " the prospects of benevolence and concord, which have seduced so many ardent minds, are, under this system, only the chimeras of the imagination. Whence should arise, in the division of labour, the determining motive to choose the most painful ? Who would undertake disagreeable and dirty tasks ? Who would be content with his lot, and not esteem the burthen of his neighbour lighter than his own ? How many frauds would be attempted in order to throw that burthen upon another, from which a man would wish to exempt himself ? and in the division of property how impossible to satisfy every one, to preserve the appearance of equality, to prevent jealousies, quarrels, rivalries, preferences ? Who shall put an end to the numberless disputes always arising ? What an apparatus of penal laws would be required, to replace the gentle liberty of choice, and the natural reward of the cares which each one takes for himself. The one half of society would not suffice to govern the other. Hence this iniquitous and absurd system could only be maintained by political or religious slavery, such as that of the Helots among the Lacedaemonians, and the Indians of Paraguay in the establishments of the Jesuits." [1]

(iv) *Malthus*

The next stage in the development of Classical thought on this subject comes with the publication of Malthus' *Essay on Population.*

[1] Bentham, *Principles of the Civil Code: op. cit.,* vol. i, p. 312. It is interesting to observe an echo of this passage in Mill's discussion of socialism, in the famous chapter on Property in his *Principles.* See below, p. 149.

In its first conception the main purpose of this essay was to examine the prospects of what the author called " the future improvement of society " in the light of the relation which he professed to have discovered between population and subsistence. This is made quite clear in the preface,[1] where the author expressly states the origin of the essay to be due to " a conversation with a friend [whom we now know to have been his father] [2] on the subject of Mr. Godwin's Essay on avarice and profusion in his Enquirer". He claims that " it is an obvious truth . . . that population must always be kept down to the level of the means of subsistence and that the means by which this is brought about constitute the strongest obstacle to any very great future improvement of society ". The purpose of the essay is therefore to make plain the nature of these means and to indicate the relevance of this discovery to the hopes of improvement which the writings of men such as Condorcet and Godwin had fostered.

The central core of the argument against hopes of perfectability was very simple : the tendency of population to press upon the limits of subsistence must necessarily frustrate these hopes. Suppose that for a brief period, improved social arrangements had brought about the abolition of poverty and distress ; even so, the growth of numbers would speedily bring such a happy state to an end. The respective powers of increase of population and subsistence being what they are, only misery and vice are capable of restraining the first to the limits imposed by the second.

This argument is developed with great vigour in the chapters especially devoted to Godwin, who had

---

[1] *Essay on Population* (1st edition, 1798), p. 1.

[2] Malthus told Pryme that this was so (Pryme, *Autobiographic Recollections*, p. 66).

ventured to predict that with the growth of enlightenment and supersession of private property by a system
of equality, an indefinite progress towards perfection
might be expected to occur.

" Let us imagine for a moment Mr. Godwin's beautiful system of equality realized in its utmost purity ",
says Malthus.[1] ". . . Let us suppose all the causes of
misery and vice in this island removed. War and contention cease. Unwholesome trades and manufactories
do not exist. Crowds no longer collect together in great
and pestilent cities for purposes of court intrigue, of
commerce and vicious gratifications. Simple, healthy,
and rational amusements take [the] place of drinking,
gaming and debauchery. . . . All men are equal. . . .
The numbers of persons and the produce of the island,
we suppose to be the same as at present. The spirit of
benevolence, guided by impartial justice, will divide this
produce among all the members of the society according
to their wants. . . .

" Let us suppose the commerce of the sexes established upon principles of the most perfect freedom. . . .
[This was a point on which Godwin laid especial stress.]
Each man would probably select himself a partner to
whom he would adhere as long as that adherence continued to be the choice of both parties. . . . Provisions
and assistance would spontaneously flow from the
quarter in which they abounded to the quarter that
was deficient. And every man would be ready to
furnish instruction to the rising generation according
to his capacity."

In such circumstances Malthus contends " with these
extraordinary encouragements to population, and every
cause of depopulation, as we have supposed, removed,
the numbers would necessarily increase faster than in

---

[1] Malthus, *op. cit.* p. 181 *seq.*

any society that has ever yet been known ". This
would be bound to lead to difficulties : a first doubling
of the population might be tolerable ; the second must
involve a descent once more to the margin of subsistence
or worse.

" Alas ! " he laments, " What becomes of the picture
where men lived in the midst of plenty : Where no man
was obliged to provide with anxiety and pain for his
restless wants : where the narrow principle of selfishness
did not exist : where Mind was delivered from her
perpetual anxiety about corporeal support, and free to
expatiate in the field of thought which is congenial to
her. This beautiful fabric of imagination vanishes at
the severe touch of truth. The spirit of benevolence,
cherished and invigorated by plenty is repressed by the
chilling breath of want. The hateful passions that had
vanished, reappear. The mighty law of self-preserva-
tion expels all the softer and more exalted emotions of
the soul. The temptations to evil are too strong for
human nature to resist. The corn is plucked before it
is ripe, or secreted in unfair proportions ; and the whole
black train of vices that belong to falsehood are immediately generated. Provisions no longer flow in for
the support of the mother with a large family. The
children are sickly from insufficient food. The rosy
flush of health gives place to the pallid cheek and hollow
eye of misery. Benevolence yet lingering in a few
bosoms, makes some faint expiring struggles, till at
length self-love resumes his wonted empire, and lords it
triumphant over the world." [1]

In such circumstances, Malthus argues, it is probable
that the institutions of property would be re-established.
" Some kind of convention would . . . be called, and
the dangerous situation of the country stated in the

[1] *Ibid.* pp. 189-190.

strongest terms." It would be represented, that in the state of disorder consequent on the scarcity of supplies, the increase of food was checked, and that in order to prevent this " it would be advisable to make a more complete division of land, and to secure every man's stock against violation by the most powerful sanctions, even by death itself ".[1] Although this might lead to inequality, this " was an evil which bore no comparison to the black train of distresses that would inevitably be occasioned by the insecurity of property. . . ."

" It seems highly probable, therefore, that an administration of property, not very different from that which prevails in civilized states at present, would be established as the best, though inadequate remedy, for the evils which were pressing on the society." [2]

Thus Malthus in the first edition of the *Essay*. Now, as we have seen,[3] in the interval between the publication of this and the preparation of the second edition, Malthus found reason to modify his views in such a manner that it seemed possible to conceive of checks to population which were neither miserable nor vicious and which permitted less pessimistic views with regard to the future of the human race. This change showed itself in many ways, from the change of title to the whole treatment of future prospects. It did not, however, influence the treatment of the systems of equality, which remained substantially unchanged throughout this and all subsequent editions.

---

[1] Malthus, *op. cit.* pp. 196-197.

[2] Lack of space prevents my reproducing the passages which describe a similar rehabilitation of marriage, but those who find a charm in the prose style of this period will find them well worth reading. They may also derive pleasure from the next chapter, the contents of which are described as follows : " Mr. Godwin's conjecture concerning the future extinction of the passion between the sexes — little apparent grounds for such a conjecture — Passion of love not inconsistent either with reason or virtue ".

[3] Lecture III above, p. 76.

The reason for this is plain. Malthus had indeed come to the conclusion that " moral restraint " might prevent population tending to outrun the limits of subsistence. But it was the essence of his argument that this check could only be expected to operate in a context of suitable institutions ; and he held firmly the view that under systems of equality and common ownership the stimulus to moral restraint would be absent.

He says this explicitly in the chapter in which he makes observations on the reply which Godwin had issued to the first edition. He points out that one of the checks to population which Godwin invokes is in effect the same as that which he himself designates as " moral restraint ", and he proceeds : " Of this check therefore itself, I entirely approve ; but I do not think that Mr. Godwin's system of political justice is by any means favourable to its prevalence. The tendency to early marriages is so strong that we want every possible help that we can get to counteract it ; and a system which in any way whatever tends to weaken the foundation of private property, and to lessen in any degree the full advantage and superiority which each individual may derive from his prudence, must remove the only counteracting weight to the passion of love, that can be depended upon for any essential effect. Mr. Godwin acknowledges that in his system ' the ill consequences of a numerous family will not come so coarsely home to each man's individual interest as they do at present '. But I am sorry to say that from what we know hitherto of the human character, we can have no rational hopes of success, without this coarse application to individual interest, which Mr. Godwin rejects." [1]

In later editions he reiterates this point. He says

---

[1] Malthus, *Essay on Population* (2nd edition, 1803), pp. 385-386. This chapter was, in subsequent editions, absorbed in the appendix.

that friends have urged him to omit the chapters dealing
with systems of equality and common ownership but he
is convinced that it is desirable that they be retained ;
and he goes on to elaborate the argument afresh in an
examination of Robert Owen's *New View of Society*.
This is very significant in this context since, of course,
Owen is specifically collectivist, whereas Godwin is so
much in the air that you never know quite where he is.[1]
But very little that is new emerges, beyond a more
concise, and perhaps even more trenchant, statement of
the result of the earlier analysis. ". . . The encouragement and motive to moral restraint are at once destroyed
in a system of equality, and community of goods . . ." [2]
The operation of the natural check to early marriage
" depends exclusively upon the existence of the laws of
property, and succession : and in a state of equality and
community of property could only be replaced by some
artificial regulation of a very different stamp and much
more unnatural character ".

(v) *The Ricardians and Robert Owen*

Between Malthus and J. S. Mill, in the literature of
Classical Economics, there is nothing on socialism which
is at all systematic. But there are incidental references
which are sufficiently revealing of the attitudes of their
authors to be worth some notice in this context.

Our main source of information regarding the attitude
of the Ricardian circle is the discussion which followed
the publication of Robert Owen's *New View of Society*
and his various proposals for absorbing unemployed

---

[1] So far as organization was concerned, Godwin was in fact anti-collectivist.
(Essay on *Political Justice* (3rd edition), vol. ii, p. 497.) It appears that he
contemplated individual production but common access to the produce.

[2] Malthus, *Essay on Population* (edited Bettany), p. 322.

labour by the organization of society in a system of
small societies — " Mr. Owen's parallelograms " as
Ricardo called them. Robert Owen was always treated
with respect by the circle. Bentham had made profitable
investments in New Lanark.[1] Ricardo, as we have seen,
defended truck because Mr. Owen practised it. Though
they made jokes about him in private and denounced his
ideas in public, their attitude was always essentially
friendly.

The *New View of Society*, together with a number of
auxiliary pamphlets, was made the subject of a full-dress
article in the *Edinburgh Review*, probably by Torrens,
and we know that the critical strictures here developed
had the full support of Ricardo, for he went out of his
way to express to Trower and others his great delight
in the way Torrens had handled the matter.[2]

Torrens' main attack on Owen's plans was on the
grounds of their complete irrelevancy. The state of
trade, he argued, was determined by the expectation
of profits ; there was nothing in the division of the

---

[1] Bentham, *op. cit.* vol. x, p. 477. This, however, did not prevent the
sage from observing to Bowring that " Robert Owen begins in vapour, and
ends in smoke " (*ibid.* p. 570).

[2] *Edinburgh Review* (1819), vol. xxxii, pp. 453-477. Contributions to the
Review were, of course, anonymous, and there has been some difference among
experts about the attribution of this particular article. The evidence in favour
of Torrens' authorship springs chiefly from a letter to McCulloch of February 28,
1820. (*Letters of Ricardo to McCulloch* (edited Hollander), p. 52.) Ricardo says,
" I was very much pleased with Col. Torrens' essay in the last *Edin. Review*.
I do not think there is more than one proposition in it which I should be disposed to dispute. Mr. Malthus was fully persuaded . . . till I undeceived him,
that the article was written by you. . . ." And in a letter to Trower of March
13, 1820 (*Letters of Ricardo to Trower* (edited Bonar and Hollander), p. 108),
he says, " Col. Torrens is becoming one of the most efficient advocates for the
right principles, as may be seen both in his review of Owen in the *Edinburgh*
and in the last edition of his work on the impolicy of restraints on the importation of corn ". [We know from a letter to Malthus of September 4, 1820
(*Letters of Ricardo to Malthus* (edited Bonar), p. 170), that the point on which he
disagreed related to the theory of gluts and not to the criticism of Owen.]
There is also strong supporting evidence in the fact that in his signed *Paper on
the Means of Reducing the Poor Rates* (London, 1817) Torrens attacks Owen
on much the same lines as those followed by the anonymous reviewer.

country into compartments of a thousand acres and the
erection in each of these of " a village in the form of a
parallelogram, with the requisite enclosures and buildings for carrying out agricultural and manufacturing
industry ", which afforded the slightest hope that the
various causes which had combined to reduce the rate of
profit would be removed, still less that the country would
thereby be enabled " to support a greatly augmented
population, in ten times the comfort enjoyed at present ".
" Our sincere esteem for the benevolent character and
disinterested conduct of Mr. Owen, withholds us from
expressing any opinion respecting the intellect of the
person who seriously proposes to accomplish such ends
by such means. His schemes do not touch, nay they
have not the most distant bearing upon the causes of
our present distress." [1]

But this does not prevent him from asking very
searching questions concerning the working of the
parallelograms. If they are to support a greatly increased population on the land, how will they avoid the
difficulties due to diminishing returns ? If they are to
be devoted to manufacture, how will they organize a
proper division of labour ? Either they will each attempt
to be self-sufficient, in which case the division of labour
will be impaired : " What should we think of the person
who should propose to increase the wealth of the country
. . . by breaking up our roads and destroying our
canals, by obstructing our rivers and closing our ports,
and by everywhere intersecting the country with im-

---

[1] *Edinburgh Review* (1819), vol. xxxii, pp. 463-464. He goes on to " en-
treat " Mr. Owen " to explain in what way the erection of villages in the form
of parallelograms could repeal those enactments against foreign trade which
are a disgrace to the age in which we live. . . . We would ask him distinctly
to state, whether he has any chance of inducing Mrs. Marcet to establish in one
of his villages a preparatory school for instructing the members of the Cabinet
in the first rudiments of economic science, and for affording them sufficient light
to retrace their ignorant and infatuated steps towards bankruptcy and ruin."

passable mountains ".[1] Or they will trade with one another and with the outside world, in which case Mr. Owen ought not to promise freedom from occasional glutting of markets and stagnation of trade " which necessarily accompany, and, in some degree, counterpoise the advantages resulting from division of employment ".[2]

Ricardo's personal concern with these schemes was of a less theoretical nature. At one stage in his propaganda Owen succeeded in acquiring the support for further investigation of his project of a large number of distinguished people including the Duke of Kent,[3] under whose auspices a mass meeting was held in the City to discuss ways and means. It appears that Ricardo, having been led by curiosity to attend this meeting in company with Torrens, found, much to his embarrassment, that he was being nominated as a member of the committee which was to decide on further action. There is an amusing letter to Trower, in which he explains his predicament. " It was in vain that I protested I differed from all the leading principles advanced by Mr. Owen, — that, I was told, was no objection, for I was not bound to approve, only to examine. With very great reluctance I at last consented, and have attended the first meeting, at which I gave my reasons at some length for departing from all Mr. Owen's conclusions. The scheme was chiefly examined with a view to a pauper establishment or a well regulated workhouse, but even to that limited plan there are insuperable objections. Owen is himself a benevolent enthusiast,

[1] *Ibid.* p. 467. [2] *Ibid.* p. 468.
[3] This was Queen Victoria's father, whose devotion to the public interest was the subject of a very famous pronouncement to Mr. Creevy. (*The Creevy Papers* (edited Maxwell), vol. i, pp. 267-271.) Owen was delighted with the association, and in his later spiritualistic phases spent many sessions in conclave with the Duke, then, of course, long since departed.

willing to make great sacrifices for a favorite object. The Duke of Kent, his great supporter, is also entitled to the praise of benevolent intentions, but he appears to me to be quite ignorant of all the principles which ought to regulate establishments for the poor — he has heard of Malthus' doctrine, and has an antipathy to it, without knowing the reasons on which it is founded or how his difficulty may be obviated. He, Mr. Preston, and Mr. Owen, appear to think nothing necessary to production, and the happiness of a crouded [sic] population, but land. We have land ; it may be made more productive, and therefore, we cannot have an excess of population. — Can any reasonable person believe, with Owen, that a society, such as he projects, will flourish and produce more than has ever yet been produced by an equal number of men, if they are to be stimulated to exertion by a regard to the community, instead of by a regard to their private interest ? Is not the experience of ages against him ? He can bring nothing to oppose to this experience but one or two ill authenticated cases of societies which prospered on a principle of a community of goods, but where the people were under the powerful influence of religious fanaticism." [1]

As might have been expected, nothing came of all this. The committee eventually recommended experimentation with schemes which had all the characteristic Owenite innovations left out ; but having failed to raise more than £8000 of the £100,000 which was considered necessary for the experiment, the project was abandoned. Nor did more come of the motion in the House of Commons of Sir W. De Crespigny for a Select Committee to inquire further into the project. Ricardo spoke on this. He made it clear that he " was completely at war with the system of Mr. Owen, which was built upon

[1] Ricardo, *Letters to Trower* (edited Bonar and Hollander), pp. 79-80.

a theory inconsistent with the principles of political economy, and in his opinion was calculated to produce infinite mischief to the community ". But he favoured the setting up of a committee as being likely to " circulate useful information and correct prejudices ".[1] Nevertheless the motion was withdrawn, and for a time nothing more was heard of the matter.

In 1823, however, in the months immediately preceding his death, Ricardo was once more preoccupied with such projects. A select committee, of which he was a member, was appointed " to inquire into conditions of labour in Ireland ", and among the witnesses called was Robert Owen, who had rehashed his parallelogram scheme to adapt it to the situation under discussion. There is no certain ground for identifying the contributions of individual members of the committee. But in view of Ricardo's specific comment on the " great attention" with which the committee had listened to Owen[2] and of his earlier association with such inquiries, it is difficult to resist connecting him both with the very severe cross-examination of Owen which is reprinted in the minutes of evidence and with the separate paragraph which the committee devotes to his scheme in their report.

The main focus both of the cross-examination and the comments in the report was the proposal for equality. It was Owen's contention that in arrangements involving complete equality of reward, production would be raised to such a point as to place the individuals concerned on a level far higher than anything attainable elsewhere. It was the contention of the committee that this was improbable — that a scheme in which " the idle and the profligate would be placed in a situation equal to that

---

[1] See *Hansard Parliamentary Debates*, vol. xli, 1206-1209. See also Cannan, *The Economic Outlook*, " Ricardo in Parliament ", p. 101.

[2] Ricardo, *Letters to Trower*, p. 207.

which would be a reward to the industrious and virtuous " would militate against efficient production. In this connexion Owen was subjected to searching examination concerning his own practice at New Lanark.

" How are the manufacturers at New Lanark paid ? — They are paid partly by day-wages, and partly by the amount of the work which they perform.

" Does a superior workman, a man of skill and ability at New Lanark, earn more than a workman of an inferior description ? — Yes ; and if the Committee will permit me, I will add that I think that one of the greatest disadvantages which exists in the establishment.

" For what reason do you conceive that to be a disadvantage ? — It is productive of inequality in a variety of ways, which in its consequences produces almost endless evils among the population ; and if the establishment were entirely my own, I would put it upon a system under which they should not receive that inequality of wages ; I should do it immediately.

" Have you ever known any establishment, or have you ever heard of any establishment carried on, in which superior skill and industry did not receive increased reward ? — Yes, I have heard of several ; there are many now existing in America.

" But you have not yourself seen any ? — I have not seen any, except the Moravians, in this country ; and there is in their establishments a mixed property, partly private and partly public : they have many of the advantages of association, and some arrangements by which individuals do partake of more advantages than others in ordinary cases.

" But in the experiment which you have tried in Lancashire and Scotland, the system of equality of profits has not yet been introduced in the payment of the manufacturers ? — It has not been yet introduced.

" Why has it not been introduced at New Lanark ? — In consequence of the arrangement at the time not being so favourable to the introduction of the system as that now proposed to be introduced. . . .

" And do you see no inconvenience from thus depriving industry, skill and character of its ordinary reward ? — Quite the reverse ; and I conceive that under this arrangement, the most inferior individuals would be very far superior to any of the same class in life that could be found in common society." [1]

The committee was evidently not impressed by these answers ; and the report, although treating Owen's intentions with the greatest respect, leaves no doubt that, in the opinion of its authors, his expectations were to be regarded as without foundation.

" When it is considered, that Mr. Owen's plan is founded upon a principle that a state of perfect equality can be produced, and can lead to beneficial consequences, Your Committee consider this position so irreconcilable with the nature and interests of mankind, and the experience of all ages, that it is impossible to treat this scheme as being practicable. . . . True it is, that Mr. Owen suggests, that under his new arrangements idleness and profligacy might be altogether extirpated from society ; but such an opinion is one which appears altogether visionary. Certainly Your Committee feel every disposition highly to estimate the effects of good education and early moral habits, but to conceive that any ' arrangement of circumstances ' can altogether divest man of his passions and frailties, as they comprehend principles in themselves undeniable, is a result which can never be anticipated.

" Your Committee will not deny, that the combination of individuals for mutual support, in establishments

---

[1] *Parliamentary Papers*, 1823, vol. vi, pp. 419-420.

conducted rather on the principles adopted at New Lanark, than upon those now suggested by Mr. Owen, might improve the habits of the people in particular districts. An economical expenditure of food and fuel ; the introduction of scientific improvements applicable to the interior of habitations ; regular employment, and good education, are all important ; but they must carefully be separated from the doctrine of community of goods and equality of profits. It does not appear to Your Committee that these causes of improvement are in any respect exclusively connected with Mr. Owen's plan ; they may flow from it so far as that plan comprehends those common principles on which all society is founded, and from whence all moral or intellectual advancement proceeds. With sincere respect therefore for the benevolence of Mr. Owen, Your Committee cannot do otherwise than dismiss his plan as impracticable, except so far as its mechanism tends to the improvement of public establishments, parish workhouses and great schools for the education of the lower classes." [1]

(vi) *Senior and the '48*

It might have been expected that the attempt by men such as Thompson and Hodgskin to build on the Ricardian system a destructive attack on capitalism would have evoked some reply from the second generation of Ricardians.[2] But it was not so. We know that they

---

[1] *Parliamentary Papers*, 1823, vol. vi, pp. 339-340.

[2] Ricardo himself had read Piercy Ravenstone's work with "great interest" although he found it " full of errors " and evidence that " the author has a very limited knowledge of the subject ". (*An Unpublished Letter of Ricardo to Malthus*, with a note by Jacob Viner, *Journal of Political Economy*, vol. xli, No. 1, February 1933, pp. 117-120). He was, of course, dead by the time Hodgskin and Thompson published their books.

regarded these attacks as pernicious. There is a very outspoken letter from James Mill to Brougham, in which he says just what he thinks of Hodgskin, whose opinions, he says, " if they were to spread, would be the subversion of civilized society : worse than the overwhelming deluge of Huns and Tartars ".[1] But in the main they did not trouble to reply.[2] We have to wait until John Stuart Mill's *Principles*, for a systematic discussion of socialist proposals.

There is, however, a further source of information concerning the attitude to socialism of this generation of economists — the diaries of Nassau Senior. Senior, as befitted the chief economic adviser of the Whigs, was as much interested in the daily evolution of policy as he was in the elaboration of general principles. In this connexion he was a fascinated observer of the French Revolution of 1848. He watched some of the events on the spot ; and

---

[1] Alexander Bain, *James Mill : a Biography*, pp. 363-367.

[2] The booklet entitled *The Rights of Industry* (London, 1831) issued, as the title-page says, " under the superintendence of the Society for the Diffusion of Useful Knowledge " and often attributed to Brougham, may perhaps be regarded as a fair statement of the probable attitude of Ricardians in this connexion ; for James Mill was a member of the committee of the Society and, as we have seen, corresponded with Brougham on matters of this sort. The booklet, which purports to show the solidarity of the interests of Capital and Labour in maintaining freedom of labour and security of property, is clearly written with Hodgskin in mind, and from time to time engages in direct polemic against him and his thesis (pp. 56-61, 191-194 and 208). As Foxwell says (Introduction to A. Menger's *Right to the Whole Produce of Labour*, p. lxxiv), it is written with skill and temperately argued : if indeed it be the work of Brougham, written amid the distractions of the Reform Bill agitation, it is yet another evidence of the versatility and power of that bewildering figure. Worth consulting in this connexion, also, is the last chapter of the second edition of the *Lectures on the Elements of Political Economy* (Columbia, 1830) by Thomas Cooper, an American economist under English Classical influence who is quoted with great approval by the author of *The Rights of Industry*. Perhaps, however, the best discussion of Hodgskin's contentions is to be found in Samuel Read's *Political Economy : An Inquiry into the Natural Grounds of Right to Vendible Property or Wealth* (Edinburgh, 1829), especially Introduction, p. xxviii, and Book I, chapter ix, section 3. But Read, of course, although strongly under the influence of Adam Smith, was not a Classical Economist in the sense in which that term is used in these lectures, being in active revolt against the most characteristic doctrines of Malthus and Ricardo.

in conversations with many of the chief participants from Alexis de Tocqueville downwards, he took endless pains to establish what he thought to be a true record of the main events and the underlying economic and political causes. In the course of his writings on this subject there occur passages which make quite explicit his own attitude to the socialistic movements of the time.[1]

Probably the most revealing of these comments occurs in the course of a *Sketch of the Revolution of 1848*, originally published in the *Edinburgh Review* from January 1850 and reprinted as an introduction to the *Journals Kept in France and Italy*. The verdict is highly unfavourable. Senior's contacts with the leading personalities and his observation of events had given him a very poor view of the motives involved and a still poorer view of the underlying theory.

Senior attributes the revolution of 1848 to a theory which he described as " a disguised socialism ". " It is the theory ", he says, " which almost every Frenchman cherishes, as respects himself — that the government exists for the purpose of making his fortune, and is to be supported only so far as it performs that duty. His great object is, to exchange the labours and risks of a business, or of a profession, or even of a trade, for a public salary. The thousands, or rather tens of thousands, of workmen who deserted employments at which they were earning four or five francs a day, to get thirty sous from the *ateliers nationaux*, were mere examples of the general feeling. To satisfy this universal desire, every

---

[1] The results of these researches are embodied, *inter alia*, in the posthumous publications edited by his daughter, M. C. M. Simpson : *Journals Kept in France and Italy from 1848 to 1852* (1871) ; *Correspondence and Conversations of Alexis de Tocqueville with Nassau William Senior from 1834 to 1859* (1872) ; *Conversation with M. Thiers, M. Guizot, and Other Distinguished Persons during the Second Empire* (1878) ; *Conversations with Distinguished Persons during the Second Empire from 1860 to 1863* (1880) — well written and entertaining works of great value for the social and political history of their time.

government goes on increasing the extent of its duties, the number of its servants, and the amount of its expenditure. . . . We do not of course believe that the great bulk of those who actually made the revolution were actuated by hope of power or of place. That the majority of the educated revolutionists were thus actuated, we have no doubt. We have no doubt that the editors and writers of the ' National ' and the ' Réforme ' intended to do precisely what they did — to make themselves the ministers, or functionaries or *protégés*, the Thiers, the Rolands, or the Mignets of a new form of government. The masses could have no such pretensions. Still they hoped to profit by a revolution ; not as individual objects of the favour of the new government, but as partakers of the blessings which the triumph of Socialism was to diffuse." [1]

The whole movement, said Senior, rested upon wrong conceptions of the power of state action. " The place-hunting of the higher orders, the socialism of the lower, the intense centralization of France, the paternal administration of Austria, arise from the same deep-rooted error as to the proper function of government. All arise from a theory that it is in the power of the State to correct the inequalities of fortune. And the error is a plausible one. Men whose reasoning faculties are either uncultivated, or perverted by their feelings or their imagination, see the great power of the State, and do not perceive its limits. They see that it disposes of great resources, and do not perceive how easily these resources may be not only exhausted, but dried up. They

[1] *Journals*, vol. i, pp. 1-5. The reader is asked to bear in mind that this is quoted as Senior's judgment, not as the verdict of the author of this essay on the train of events involved. Those who find it an unexpectedly harsh verdict from one who was undoubtedly a liberal rather than a conservative in his general outlook, should refer to the even more drastic comments of Bagehot, reporting to the *Economist* the background of the *coup d'état* of Louis-Napoleon. (The reports are reprinted in the Everyman edition of his *Literary Studies*.)

are struck by the contrast between great superfluity and great indigence, between lives shortened by indolence and lives shortened by toil, by wealth squandered unproductively while cultivable lands lie waste and labourers ask in vain for employment. When excited by such a spectacle, what is more natural than to propose laws, by which the toil which appears to them excessive shall be forbidden, by which the government shall provide the strong with employment and the weak with relief ; and obtain the necessary funds, partly from the superfluity of the rich, and partly by taking possession of the productive instruments which their present owners are too idle or too timid to turn to the best advantage ? It requires a long train of reasoning to show that the capital on which the miracles of civilization depend is the slow and painful creation of the economy and enterprise of the few and of the industry of the many, and is destroyed, or driven away, or prevented from arising, by any causes which diminish or render insecure the profits of the capitalist, or deaden the activity of the labourer ; and that the State, by relieving idleness, improvidence, or misconduct from the punishment, and depriving abstinence and foresight of the rewards, which have been provided for them by nature, may indeed destroy wealth, but most certainly will aggravate poverty."

Senior was especially impressed by the dangers, as he conceived them, of the guarantee of employment and the fiasco of the *Ateliers Nationaux*.

As regards the former, he quoted with warm approval Tocqueville's " great speech " on the *droit au travail*. " If the State [says M. de Tocqueville] attempts to fulfil its engagement by itself giving work, it becomes itself a great employer of labour. As it is the only capitalist that cannot refuse employment, and as it is the capitalist whose workpeople are always the most lightly tasked, it will soon become the greatest, and soon after the only great, employer. The public revenue, instead of merely supporting the government will have to support all the industry of the country. As rents and profits are swallowed up by taxes, private property, now become a mere incumbrance, will be abandoned to the State ; and subject to the duty of maintaining the people, the government will be the only proprietor. This is Communism.

" If, on the other hand the State, in order to escape from this train of consequences, does not itself find work, but takes care that it shall always be supplied by individual capitalists, it must take care that at no place and at no time there be a stagnation. It must take on itself the management of both capitalists and labourers. It must see that the one class do not injure one another by over trading, or the other by competition. It must regulate profits and wages — sometimes retard, sometimes accelerate, production or consumption. In short, in the jargon of the school, it must organize industry. This is Socialism." [1]

The guarantee of employment, Senior argued, involved necessarily the creation of the *Ateliers Nationaux*. The failure of these could be explained in terms of general principle. In the free individualistic society industry is maintained by the connexion between effort and output. Under slavery, it is enforced by punishment. " But in eleemosynary employment there is absolutely no motive for the labourer to make any exertion, or for the employer, a mere public officer, to enforce it. The labourer is, at all events, to have subsistence for himself and his family. To give him more would immediately attract to the public paymaster all the labourers of the country ; to give him less, and yet require his services, would be

1 Senior, *op. cit.* pp. 52-53.

both cruelty and fraud. He cannot be discharged — he cannot be flogged — he cannot be put to task work — since to apportion the tasks to the various powers of individuals would require a degree of zealous and minute superintendence which no public officer ever gave."

Senior was quite willing to admit that the lack of employment in Paris, due to the alarm caused by the revolution, may have necessitated extraordinary action in the form of relief. The mistake of the revolutionary government in his judgment did not lie there but rather in the guarantee of employment. " Had not that decree been issued, relief to the unemployed would have been given *as* relief." But the decree made that impossible. " The decree guaranteed employment — not to the diligent or to the well disposed, but to all. Now to guarantee *subsistence* to all [here spoke the author of the New Poor Law of 1834] — to proclaim that no man whatever his vices or even his crimes, shall die of hunger or cold — is a promise that in the state of civilization of England, or of France can be performed not merely with safety but with advantage, because the gift of mere subsistence may be subjected to conditions which no one will voluntarily accept. But *employment* cannot safely be made degrading, and cannot practically be made more severe." [1]

These passages — and it would be possible to cite

---

[1] *Op. cit.* pp. 57-58. Doubtless Senior had been influenced by a conversation with Horace Say (recorded on page 103 of vol. i of the *Journals*), in which he was told that " the promise made by the Provisional Government of employment at good wages has sunk deep into the minds of the people, and renders poor law on the English system — that of affording relief on terms less acceptable than wages — impossible ". On this particular subject it is interesting to observe that J. S. Mill held more or less the same view as Senior. " If the state or the parish provides ordinary work, at ordinary wages, for all the unemployed, the work so provided cannot be made less desirable, and can scarcely be prevented from being more desirable than any other employment. It would therefore become necessary, either that the state should arbitrarily limit its operations (in which case no material advantage would arise from their having been commenced), or that it should be willing to take the whole productive industry

several others [1] — leave no room for doubt concerning Senior's attitude to socialism, as it had been propounded up to 1848. He thought that the analysis on which it was based was faulty ; and that the actual measures and institutions proposed were likely to be attended by bad results. He summed up this attitude in his Oxford lectures of 1848-9 : " Even plunder or confiscation is less fatal to abstinence than what is called socialism or communism. The first only incidentally diminish the motives to production, the second aims specifically at destroying them. It proposes to enact that industry shall not be rewarded by wages nor abstinence by profit : that those who toil shall toil for others and those who save shall save for others — in short that hope shall cease to govern mankind. If this system should ever be attempted to be adopted — and I do not think the possibility of the experiment's being made can be denied — it will be necessary to substitute fear, and the socialist nation, unless it is to starve, must be divided into slaves and slavedrivers." [2]

of the country under the direction of its own officers." (*Letters of John Stuart Mill* (edited Hugh Elliot), vol. i, p. 152). In some future age, he thinks, perhaps the latter alternative may be possible, but in present circumstances it is out of the question. Hence the enforcement of the " right to labour " is inexpedient.

[1] *E.g.* Senior, *op. cit.* pp. 150, 169 and 276.

[2] The passage comes from Mr. Levy's compilation of extracts from Senior's various writings, published and unpublished, entitled *Industrial Efficiency and Social Economy*, vol. i, pp. 212-213. A straight publication of Senior's unpublished Oxford lectures is one of the main *desiderata* of the scholarship of Classical Economics.

THE CLASSICAL ECONOMISTS AND SOCIALISM: JOHN STUART MILL

(i) *Introduction*

So far, in the course of this last investigation, our material has been inferential or episodic. It has been possible to build up a more or less coherent picture of the probable attitude of the English Classical Economists to the challenge of socialist ideas. But we have not discovered any comprehensive or balanced analysis. The early Classical Economists were much too preoccupied with pushing their own reforms to regard the current socialism as anything but a side issue. Even when it had attained sufficient ascendancy to influence political action, as in France in 1848, the disposition, which we see very clearly exemplified by Senior, was to dismiss it as essentially half-baked and wrong-headed.

When we come to John Stuart Mill, however, we find a very different mode of treatment and a very different habit of mind. Here we find a definite attempt at systematic and detached consideration. Here, too, we find an emotional attitude which, to put it at its lowest, was certainly not hostile. There can indeed be no doubt that, whatever his ultimate conclusions (which, as we shall see, are not at all easy to disentangle), with one part of his being John Stuart Mill would have dearly liked to believe in socialism in some form or other. There is no argument with socialists *de haut en bas* where

he is concerned : indeed he often takes the most pre-
posterous people much more seriously than they deserve
— witness, for instance, his continual harking back to
Fourier who thought, among other things, that, under
socialism, living creatures inimical to man could be
turned into their opposite, instead of the lion the " anti-
lion ", etc. etc. Although so superior in integrity and
intellectual power to most that we seem able to produce
to-day, in many ways Mill is a typical modern : he was
unsettled about the fundamental basis of society ; in
spite of his belief in progress he was afraid of the future ;
he did not feel confident that he knew where we were
going ; what is more, he did not feel quite confident that
he knew where he wanted us to go. For these reasons,
and because, from that day to this, there has been much
misunderstanding of what Mill's attitude finally amounted
to, it is worth examining his views at some length.[1]

To do this with understanding it is necessary to keep
in mind certain of Mill's general characteristics, which
are not infrequently forgotten.

First, his strong emotions. The great mid-Victorian
intellectual who dominated his generation of progressives
by the sheer power of disinterested thought was, in fact,
a man of intense and sometimes overpowering feelings.

---

[1] In this investigation I have not found much help in the existing literature.
Mill has been claimed as the arch-individualist by some, as a good socialist by
others. I had hoped to get some assistance from the work of Jean Lubac,
John Stuart Mill et le socialisme (Paris, 1902), but the author, although setting
out with great clarity the systematic conception he has formed, seems entirely
anaesthetic to the important differences between the chapters in the third
and subsequent editions of the *Principles* and the *Posthumous Chapters on
Socialism* ; moreover, he makes little attempt to ask what type of socialism
was really in Mill's mind, as if this was not a very critical matter. Ashley's
Appendix K to his edition of the *Principles* is much more helpful. My difficulty
with him is that I suspect that he makes the contrast too striking, not by
bringing out the very sceptical nature of the *Chapters* — that is so unmistakable
that it cannot seriously be called in question — but rather by an implicit over-
emphasis on the positive content, as distinct from the mood of the changes in
the third edition of the *Principles*. But on all this see below, p. 165 *seq.*

This may not leap to the eye from the general nature of his speculative preoccupations. But it is plain enough in the *Autobiography*, and elsewhere it is not hard to find : not only the *Liberty* and the *Subjection of Women*, but the *Political Economy* and even the *Logic* are inspired by an emotional force which the deliberate systematization of the argument and the somewhat heavy structure of the sentences only very imperfectly conceal.

These emotions, however, were not altogether assimilated to the other elements in his personality. The unnatural nature of his upbringing, the emotional starvation of his childhood and early manhood, brought it about that when at last this side of his personality was allowed to develop, it retained a certain awkwardness, a certain alternation of inhibition and disproportionate expression, in sharp contrast to the maturity of his capacity for logical analysis. The circumstances attending the great passion of his life for Harriet Taylor, who afterwards became his wife, doubtless aggravated these tendencies, particularly where she was concerned.[1]

Finally, and in my judgment most important of all, we must note his constant tendency to exaggerate his differences with his predecessors. In spite of his nearness to them, John Stuart Mill is by no means always a good interpreter of the earlier generation of utilitarians. The reason for this is not far to seek. The nature of his mental crisis and the means whereby he nursed himself back to spiritual health all involved a break with family influences which he associated with early utilitarianism ; far more than was intellectually justifiable, he tended to identify Benthamism and the Classical system with his father, James Mill. There was a period in his life when he

---

[1] On this episode, so important for the history of thought as well as for Mill's personal history, see F. A. Hayek, *John Stuart Mill and Harriet Taylor : Their Correspondence and Subsequent Marriage.*

definitely disavowed connexion with the movement, although this did not last. The result was that, feeling detached in emotion, he tended to believe himself to be also detached in intellectual outlook, to emphasize differences and to magnify the importance for him of opposing schools of thought ; his tribute to Coleridge is a case in point.[1] Now there were real differences, not merely of feeling and outlook but also of intellectual conviction ; it would be wrong to suggest that these were negligible. Yet, in the last analysis, if we look at what he actually said, the similarities seem much more significant than the dissimilarities : there was something in his make-up which, when all the protestations were over, usually pulled him back to intellectual continuity. In spite of all the disclaimers of his middle period, he remained a great Utilitarian and a great exponent of Classical Political Economy.

But enough of these general observations. Their relevance will, I hope, become clear as we address ourselves to the difficult task of examining the various phases of Mill's attitude to the socialism of his day.

(ii) *J. S. Mill and the Saint-Simonians*

The first of these phases comes in the period following his first great emotional crisis.

---

[1] It is interesting to compare his attitude with De Quincey's in this respect. De Quincey was, of course, a much smaller man, at any rate as a social philosopher. But being, what Mill was certainly not, more than half a poet himself, he was able to evaluate just as well as Mill the magic of Coleridge's poetry and to be much more aware of the vein of pure hot air and pseudo-wisdom in the Coleridgean attitude to society. Anyone wishing to form a correct judgment of the extent of Coleridge's contribution in this respect, should certainly take note of Mill's masterly systematization thereof in his famous essay on this subject (*Dissertations and Discussions*, vol. i) ; but he should not neglect to apply some corrective by consulting De Quincey on the attitude of the Lake Poets to Political Economy ; it was a matter on which De Quincey had much more insight and much more personal experience. *Reminiscences of the English Lake Poets* (Everyman edition, pp. 194-199).

" The writers by whom, more than by any others, a new mode of political thinking was brought home to me," he says, " were those of the St.-Simonian school in France. . . . I was kept *au courant* of their progress by one of their most enthusiastic disciples, M. Gustave d'Eichtal, who about that time passed a considerable interval in England. I was introduced to their chiefs, Bazard and Enfantin in 1830 ; and, as long as their public teachings and proselytism continued, I read nearly everything they wrote. Their criticisms on the common doctrines of Liberalism seemed to me full of important truth ; and it was partly by their writings that my eyes were opened to the very limited and temporary value of the old political economy, which assumes private property and inheritance as indefeasible facts, and freedom of production and exchange as the *dernier mot* of social improvement." [1]

For the time being, Mill became almost St.-Simonian. Writing long after, when the sect had dissolved and its leaders had long since gone off to the east, first to find the ideal woman and then to help in the cutting of the Suez Canal, Mill saw difficulties which, as we shall see, led him to speak of their assumptions as " almost too chimerical to be reasoned against ".[2] But, at the time, he was able to write to d'Eichtal, " I am now inclined to believe that your social organization under some modification or other — which experience will, no doubt, one day suggest to yourselves — is likely to be the final and permanent condition of the human race. I chiefly differ from you in thinking that it will require many, or at least several ages to bring mankind into a state in which they will be capable of it. . . . " [3]

[1] J. S. Mill, *Autobiography* (World's Classics edition), pp. 138, 141.
[2] See below, p. 151.
[3] *Letters of John Stuart Mill* (edited Elliot), vol. i, p. 20.

And in the *Autobiography*, writing still later than the condemnation quoted above, he explains that " the scheme gradually unfolded by the St.-Simonians, under which the labour and the capital of society would be managed for the general account of the community, every individual being required to take a share of labour, either as thinker, teacher, artist or producer, all being classed according to their capacity, and remunerated according to their work, appeared to me a far superior description of socialism to Owen's. Their aim seemed to me desirable and rational, however their means might be inefficacious ; and [here we find something not altogether easy to square with the letter to d'Eichtal] though I neither believed in the practicability, nor in the beneficial operation of their social machinery, I felt that the proclamation of such an ideal of human society could not but tend to give a beneficial direction to the efforts of others to bring society, as at present constituted, nearer to some ideal standard." [1]

Thus in the early thirties, whether or not he believed in " the beneficial operation of their social machinery ", Mill was decidedly under the influence of this quite definitely socialist school of thought.

(iii) *The First Edition of the* Principles

When we come to the first edition of the *Principles*, however, and examine the discussion of socialism which is there to be found in the chapter on *Property*, we find a frame of mind and a point of view which certainly appear to be very different. This chapter deserves special attention ; it is here that we find what Mill obviously then thought to be a systematic and well-balanced treatment : and it is here that, in the third

[1] J. S. Mill, *Autobiography* (World's Classics edition), pp. 141-142.

edition, there take place those very substantial changes which by some have been taken to authorize the use of his name as a positive supporter of socialism in the modern sense.

The argument of the first edition is not very extensive and its conclusion is not at all favourable to the proposals under discussion.

If private property were not permitted, says Mill, then " the plan which must be adopted would be to hold the land and all instruments of production as the joint property of the community, and to carry on the operations of industry on the common account. . . ."[1] " In an age like the present, when a general reconsideration of all first principles is felt to be inevitable, and when for the first time in history the most suffering portions of the community have a voice in the discussion, it was impossible but that ideas of this nature should spread far and wide. Owenism, or Socialism, in this country, and Communism on the Continent, are the most prevalent forms of the doctrine."

Now, argues Mill, it would be too much to affirm that small communities of this sort could not work at a not intolerable level of well-being. It is not easy to conceive a country of any large extent forming a single " cooperative society ". But there might be a number of small communities which had a congress to settle their joint affairs. " Supposing that the soil and climate were tolerably propitious, and that the several communities, possessing the means of all necessary production within themselves, had not to contend in the general markets of the world against the competition of societies founded on private property, I doubt not that by a very rigid system of repressing population, they might be able to live and hold together, without discomfort." It is

[1] *Principles of Political Economy* (1st edition), vol. i, p. 239 *seq.*

possible, he thinks, to overstate the extent to which anti-social conduct would endanger the minimum standard ; armies are run without the incentive of gain, yet reasonable obedience to duty is secured.

But it is difficult to believe that such societies could rise much above the minimum. " In the long run, little more work would be performed by any than could be exacted from all ", and it is to be feared that " the standard of industrial duty would, therefore, be fixed extremely low ". Invention might go on because that may be pleasant in itself. But the carrying out of invention, which is often a dull and toilsome task, would probably suffer from the indifference of the majority.

Moreover, " the perfect equality contemplated in the theory of the scheme could not be really attained. The produce might be divided equally but how could the labour ? " In the competitive system labour is distributed between different occupations with some approach to fairness. This is marred by obstacles to mobility and inequality of opportunity, but it is possible to hope that, as time goes on, those will disappear. But " on the Communist system the impossibility of making the adjustment between different qualities of labour is so strongly felt, that the advocates of the scheme usually find it necessary to provide that all should work by turns at every description of useful labour : an arrangement which, by putting an end to the division of employments, would sacrifice the principal advantage which co-operative production possesses, and would probably reduce the amount of production still lower than in our supposition. And after all, the nominal equality of labour would be so great a real inequality, that justice would revolt at its being enforced."

But supposing these difficulties surmounted, Mill

still doubts whether the gain would be great. The uncertainty regarding the means of subsistence would be absent. But this is not a very great positive good; and "there is little attractive in a monotonous routine, without vicissitudes, but without excitement; a life spent in the enforced observance of an external rule, and performance of a prescribed task : in which labour would be devoid of its chief sweetener, the thought that every effort tells perceptibly on the labourer's own interests or those of someone with whom he identifies himself . . . in which no one's way of life, occupation, or movements, would depend on choice, but each would be the slave of all. . . ." Perhaps it is true that, for the majority, such a condition would not be radically different from the life they now lead. But for the rest the position would be worse. "I believe", says Mill, "that the conditions of the operatives in a well regulated manufactory . . . is very like what the condition of all would be in a socialist community. I believe that the majority would not exert themselves for anything beyond this, and that unless they did, nobody else would; and that on this basis human life would settle itself into one invariable round." But finally even this state of affairs could not be sustained without public regulation of propagation, since "prudential restraint would no longer exist". But an equal degree of regulation could secure equal results under the present system ; and there would still be elbow-room for the energetic. "Whatever of pecuniary means or freedom of action any one obtained beyond this, would be so much to be counted in favour of the competitive system. It is an abuse of the principle of equality to demand that no individual be permitted to be better off than the rest, when his being so makes none of the others worse off than they otherwise would be."

Such arguments, Mill thinks, weigh heavily against communism. They do not apply to St.-Simonism, which does not propose such a wooden system of equality and which acknowledges the need for direction by people of superior qualities. But St.-Simonism has difficulties of its own. " It supposes an absolute despotism in the heads of the association ", and " to suppose that one or a few human beings, however selected could . . . be qualified to adapt each person's work to his capacity and proportion each person's remuneration to his merits . . .", " or that any use which they could make of this power would give general satisfaction, or would be submitted to without the aid of force — is a supposition almost too chimerical to be reasoned against ".

Hence we are not surprised when Mill returns to the property principle as the best basis of organization and to urge that " It is not the subversion of the system of individual property that should be aimed at ; but the improvement of it, and the participation of every member of the community in its benefits ". We know from Alexander Bain that he attached great importance to his proposals in this respect.[1]

(iv) *The Third Edition of the* Principles

Thus the first edition ; at this stage the verdict on socialism is apparently adverse. In the third edition,[2] however, there are extensive changes which are signalled

[1] " What I remember most vividly of his talk pending the publication of the work, was his anticipating a tremendous outcry about his doctrines on Property. He frequently spoke of his proposals as to Inheritance and Bequest, which if carried out would pull down all large fortunes in two generations. To his surprise, however, this part of the book made no sensation " (Bain, *J. S. Mill*, p. 89).

[2] There are some changes in the second edition ; Mill had already become apprehensive lest his critique should have gone too far. But it is the changes in the third edition which are outstanding.

in the Preface in these terms : " The chapter on Property has been almost entirely rewritten. I was far from intending that the statement which it contained, of the objections to the best known Socialist schemes, should be understood as a condemnation of Socialism, regarded as an ultimate result of human progress. The only objection to which any great importance will be found to be attached in the present edition is the unprepared state of mankind in general, and of the labouring classes in particular. . . . It appears to me that the great end of social improvement should be to fit mankind by cultivation for a state of society combining the greatest personal freedom with that just distribution of the fruits of labour which the present laws of property do not profess to aim at. Whether, when this state of mental and moral cultivation shall be attained, individual property in some form (though in a form very remote from the present) or community of ownership in the instruments of production and a regulated division of the produce, will afford the circumstances most favourable to happiness . . . is a question which must be left, as it safely may, to the people of that time to decide. Those of the present are not competent to decide it."

The modifications of the text are indeed considerable.[1]

First, the argument that under socialism it would be improbable that productivity would rise above a somewhat low level is whittled away. It is admitted that the absence of a direct connexion between reward and effort would have disadvantages. But it is urged that there is a similar absence of incentive where time wages or fixed salaries prevail in the individualistic society ; and it is urged that it is possible that the growth of public spirit would diminish these disadvantages. " Mankind are capable of a far greater amount of public spirit

---

[1] *Principles of Political Economy* (3rd edition), vol. i, pp. 243-263.

than the present age is accustomed to suppose possible."
The pressure of public opinion and the power of emula-
tion might do far more than they do at present. To
what extent, therefore, the energy of labour would be
diminished by communism, or whether in the long run it
would be diminished at all, must be considered for the
present an undecided question.

Secondly, the Malthusian argument is withdrawn.
There is really a total *volte-face* here. "Communism is
precisely the state of things in which opinion might be
expected to declare itself with greatest intensity against
this kind of selfish intemperance." A fall in productivity
due to an increase in numbers could not be attributed
to the avarice of employers or the unjust privileges of the
rich. If public opinion were not sufficient, then "pen-
alties of some description" could be trusted to keep
population in check.

The difficulties of apportioning labour among different occupations continue to be recognized. But it is
urged that such difficulties "though real, are not insuperable". We are exhorted to remember that the
difficulties of communism are at present much better
understood than its resources ; and that the intellect of
mankind is only beginning to contrive the means of
organizing it in detail, so as to overcome the one and
derive the greatest advantage from the other.

Such reasonings lead to the dramatic outburst : "If
the choice were to be made between Communism with all
its chances, and the present state of society (1852) with all
its sufferings and injustices ; if the institution of private
property necessarily carried with it as a consequence,
that the produce of labour should be apportioned as we
now see it, almost in an inverse ratio to the labour —
the largest portions to those who have never worked at
all, the next largest to those whose work is almost

nominal, and so on in a descending scale, the remuneration dwindling as the work grows harder and more disagreeable, until the most fatiguing and exhausting bodily
labour cannot count with certainty on being able to earn
even the necessaries of life ; if this, or Communism, were
the alternative, all the difficulties, great or small, of
Communism, would be as dust in the balance ".

But they are not the alternatives. " To make the
comparison applicable, we must compare Communism
at its best, with the regime of private property, not as it
is, but as it might be made." Then follows the passage
which I have quoted already at an earlier stage,[1] which
argues that the principle of private property has not
yet had a fair trial. Assume that private property
could be reformed, assume too that there is universal
education and a due restraint of numbers, assumptions
which are equally necessary if communism is to be regarded as workable, then " there could be no poverty
even under the present social institutions : and . . . the
question of Socialism is not, as generally stated by
Socialists, a question of flying to the sole refuge against
the evils which now bear down humanity ; but a mere
question of comparative advantages which futurity must
determine ".

Even in this context, however, if I am not mistaken,
the scales are not left quite in this even position. The
future author of *Liberty* could not wholly suppress some
slight apprehension regarding the degree of freedom
under communism. " If a conjecture may be hazarded,"
he allows himself to say, " the decision will probably
depend mainly on one consideration, viz. which of the
two systems is consistent with the greatest amount of
human liberty and spontaneity . . . it remains to be
discovered how far the preservation of this characteristic

---

[1] Lecture II above, pp. 64-65.

would be found compatible with the Communistic organization of society." At once, he adds that "no doubt, this, like all the other objections to the Socialist schemes, is vastly exaggerated. . . . The restraints of Communism would be freedom in comparison with the present condition of the majority of the human race." But then again, "it is not by comparison with the present sad state of society that the claims of Communism can be estimated ; nor is it sufficient that it should promise greater personal and mental freedom than is now enjoyed by those who have not enough of either to deserve the name. The question is whether there would be any asylum left for individuality of character; whether public opinion would not be a tyrannical yoke ; whether the absolute dependence of each on all, the surveillance of each by all, would not grind all down into a tame uniformity of thoughts, feelings and actions. This is already one of the glaring evils of the existing state of Society, notwithstanding a much greater diversity of education and pursuits, and a much less absolute dependence of the individual on the mass, than would exist in a communistic régime. No Society in which eccentricity is a matter of reproach, can be in a wholesome state. It has yet to be ascertained whether the Communistic scheme would be favourable to the multiform development of human nature." The nuance of phrase here seems to shade into a certain anxious scepticism.

What does all this mean ? And to what extent is it to be regarded as Mill's settled judgment on these matters ?

There is no doubt at all that, from Mill's point of view, the change of emphasis was a change which he took very seriously. In one of the most famous passages in the *Autobiography* [1] Mill explains the evolution of his

---

[1] *Op. cit.* pp. 195-196.

ideas, from his early position of " extreme Benthamism "
when " private property, as now understood, and inheritance, appeared to me . . . the *dernier mot* of
legislation ",[1] to a position in which he and his wife
regarded " all existing institutions and social arrangements as being . . . ' merely provisiõnal ' and welcomed
with the greatest pleasure and interest all Socialistic experiments by select individuals. . . ." In this state of
mind, he says, " We were now much less democrats
than I had been, because so long as education continues
to be so wretchedly imperfect, we dreaded the ignorance
and especially the selfishness and brutality of the
mass : but our ideal of ultimate improvement went far
beyond Democracy, and would class us decidedly
under the general designation of Socialists ". And he
explains how such opinions came to be promulgated
" less clearly and fully in the first ", but " quite unequivocally in the third ", edition of the *Principles of
Political Economy*.

This explanation is not altogether easy to follow.
The preponderance of argument in the first edition seems
definitely against socialism, whereas in the third the
balance is almost completely even. The continuity of
thought, which Mill assumes, seems to be, in fact, much
more only some continuity of feeling. But about the
degree of openness of mind and judgment expressed in
the third edition, there can be no serious question. The
main obstacle to socialism — whatever that may prove

---

[1] This passage illustrates very well Mill's occasional tendency, when referring
to the ideas from which he revolted, to over-simplify and distort. There is no
need to question the assertion that at that time he himself accepted private
property and inheritance *simpliciter*, and could conceive no way of mitigating
their consequences other than by abolishing primogeniture and entails. But this
is not true of the attitude of Bentham. (See above, Lecture III, p. 64.) Mill
knew this and referred to Bentham's proposals in this connexion in his *Principles*.
But such was the force of his emotional recoil from his early background that
he seldom could resist the impulse, doubtless quite unconscious, to over-
simplify and to make the contrast greater than it actually was.

to mean — is now conceived to be only the backward
state of morals and education ; and as, marvellous to
relate, Mill genuinely believed his own intellectual
eminence and public spirit to be due entirely to the
education he had received from his father,[1] it is not
difficult to understand how he came to conceive that in
some future age, the benefits of education having become
more or less universally diffused, this obstacle to the
realization of his ideal might be removed.

Nevertheless, if we are to gauge correctly the significance of the change, it is very important that we should
realize the nature of the conceptions to which it referred
and the degree of emphasis which it implied.   In this
connexion, I submit, it is most important to interpret
the chapter on *Property* in the closest conjunction with
the chapter *On the Probable Future of the Labouring
Classes.* We know that this latter was a chapter to
which Mill attached very special importance.   It was
the chapter whose inclusion had been suggested by Mrs.
Taylor and " the more general part of the chapter . . .",
according to Mill, " was wholly an exposition of her
thoughts, often in words taken from her lips ".[2]

Now this chapter, although rewritten and extended,
underwent far fewer vicissitudes in its general viewpoint
between the first edition and the third. The opening para-
graphs, with their splendid formulation of the contrast

---

[1] The passage in which this belief is set forth has to be read to be believed :
" If I had been by nature extremely quick of apprehension or had possessed
a very accurate and retentive memory, or were of a remarkably active and
energetic character, the trial would not be conclusive : but in all these natural
gifts I am rather below than above par : what I could do, could assuredly
be done by any boy or girl of average capacity and healthy physical constitution : and if I have accomplished anything, I owe it, among other fortunate circumstances, to the fact that through the early training bestowed on
me by my father, I started, I may fairly say, with an advantage of a quarter of
a century over my contemporaries " (*Autobiography* (World's Classics edition),
p. 26).   In other words, any ordinary child if subjected to a similar training could
have become a John Stuart Mill !

[2] *Ibid.* p. 208.

between " the theory of dependence and protection "
and " the theory of self-dependence ", remained broadly
unchanged. (If these were really Mrs. Taylor's, it is
not so difficult to understand something of Mill's gratitude and admiration.) And although much was added
to the latter part of the chapter by way of examples of
successful co-partnership and elaboration of the possibilities of full co-operative production, the tone and
purpose of the general vision of the future remained
substantially the same.

What was this vision ? This can be best stated in the
words of the definitive edition, not greatly changed from
those inserted in the third. " Hitherto there has been
no alternative for those who lived by their labour, but
that of labouring either each for himself alone or for a
master. But the civilizing and improving influences of
association, and the efficiency and economy of production on a large scale, may be obtained without dividing
the producers into two parties with hostile interests and
feelings, the many who do the work being mere servants
under the command of the one who supplies the funds,
and having no interest of their own in the enterprise
except to earn their wages with as little labour as
possible. The speculations and discussions of the last
fifty years, and the events of the last thirty, are abundantly conclusive on this point. If the improvement
which even triumphant military despotism has only re-
tarded, not stopped, shall continue its course, there can
be little doubt that the *status* of hired labourers will
gradually tend to confine itself to the description of
workpeople whose low moral qualities render them unfit
for anything more independent : and that the relation
of masters and workpeople will gradually be superseded
by partnership in one of two forms : in some cases
association of the labourers with the capitalist ; in

others, and perhaps finally in all, association of labourers among themselves." [1]

This passage is surely very important. For if it means anything at all it must mean that the " Socialism " which Mill had in mind in the *Autobiography* as possibly ultimately desirable, was not a centralized organization with an all-powerful state owning and running the means of production, distribution and exchange, but rather a congeries of co-operative bodies of workers practising the virtues of association among themselves but independent, in the same sense in which any part of a social organism can be independent *vis-à-vis* other members of society. That is to say, that the desirable future for the labouring classes lay more in a *syndicalist* rather than a *collectivist* direction. I am not arguing that this was necessarily sensible. I think indeed that it is perhaps proof of the very considerable naïveté of Mill's outlook that he did not feel under any obligation at this point to discuss the mutual relations of these co-operative associations of the future ; for unless there is some solution of this problem the whole question of allocation of resources remains completely unsolved. [2] But I do suggest that realization that this was the ultimate nature

---

[1] *Principles* (Ashley's edition), pp. 763-764.

[2] There is no discussion at all in the *Principles* of the pricing problem under socialism, nor any recognition of its importance. But in a review of Francis Newman's *Lectures on Political Economy* (*Westminster Review*, LVI, 83-101, October 1851), there is some allusion to it. Newman had accused socialism of " blindness to the fact, that there can be no such thing as price, except through the influence of competition ; nor, therefore, without competition, can there be any exchanges between community and community." On this Mill comments, " Socialists would reply, that they propose that exchanges between community and community should be at cost price. If it were asked how the cost price is to be ascertained, they would answer, that in the operations of communities, every element of cost would be a matter of public record ; so that every dealer, on the private system, is required and able to ascertain what price will remunerate him for his goods, and the agents of the communities would only be required to do the same thing. This would be, no doubt, one of the practical difficulties, and we think it somewhat undervalued by them ; but the difficulty cannot be insurmountable."

of Mill's utopia makes it much easier to understand why in the convenient ambiguity of terminology which then prevailed, he found it possible to designate himself as a socialist. There is nothing in his work which would suggest that he would have viewed with favour a centralized collectivism on a large scale. All his libertarian supicions were already aroused by the projects of the St.-Simonians. He had had his disillusionment with Comte, of whose later work he was subsequently to say that it stood " a monumental warning to thinkers on society and politics, of what happens when once men lose sight in their speculations of the value of Liberty and of Individuality " ; [1] and Comte, although not a socialist in the ordinary sense of the word, had come from the St.-Simonian stable. But if " socialism " could include the idyllic plan of a society of co-operative associations of workers — superior versions of M. Leclaire's benefi- cent experiment — then he might be well content to be regarded as a socialist. In the light of the problems of a modern machine society, the logic of the syndicalist solu- tion may seem somewhat inadequate — has it indeed ever recovered from the damage inflicted by the mock slogan devised by the Webbs, " The sewers for the sewage men " ? But Mill is very typical. It is this vision of the future, rather than that of central collectivism, which has usually captured the fancy of lovers of liberty who, for one reason or another, have wished to transcend the society based on private property and the market.

(v) *The Posthumous Chapters on Socialism*

Our problems, however, are not yet at an end. The revisions in the third edition of the *Principles* and the

---

[1] *Autobiography* (World's Classics edition), pp. 180-181.

passages in those parts of the *Autobiography* last revised in 1861, are not the final sources for Mill's ultimate views on socialism.

Very late in life, Mill began to draw up a more systematic statement of his position. This was never finished ; but after his death the fragment of a draft was published in the *Fortnightly Review* by the authority of Helen Taylor, who may safely be trusted not to have released to the world anything which she regarded as misrepresenting her stepfather's views. As we shall see, these chapters themselves raise new problems of interpretation. But they are of critical importance in enabling us to assess Mill's final position on the problems with which they deal.

The fragment falls into three main parts, the arrangement of which may convey some suggestion of an underlying attitude of mind. In the first part Mill states as strongly as he can the case made by contemporary socialists against the individualist society ; in the second, he corrects what he regards as certain weaknesses in this case — the belief in a falling level of real wages, fallacious views regarding competition, misapprehensions regarding the magnitude of profits. In the third, he sets forth " the difficulties of Socialism " and concludes with emphasis on the variability of the institution of property. For our purposes, it is this last section which is chiefly relevant.

Mill begins by making a distinction between types of socialists : on the one hand, " the more thoughtful and philosophic Socialists ", " whose plans for a new order of society . . . are on the scale of a village community or township and would be applied to an entire country by the multiplication of such self-acting units ", on the other hand, the revolutionary socialists, " more a product of the Continent than of Great Britain ", whose

" scheme is the management of the whole productive resources of the country by one central authority, the general government. . . . Whatever be the difficulties of the first of these . . . the second must evidently involve the same difficulties and many more." He therefore proposes to discuss them in this order.

So far as the first type of socialism is concerned, the discussion follows much the same order as that of the chapter on *Property* in the *Principles*. But its general tone is much less favourable. The discussion of incentive now seems to tip the scales definitely in a direction adverse to socialism. As regards the mass of the workers, Mill thinks, it is difficult to believe that they would do better than workers paid by time under capitalism and not as well as workers paid by piece or associated with the success of their firm by profit-sharing or co-partnership ; while the incentive to good management would be less. " It thus appears that as far as concerns the motives to exertion in the general body, Communism has no advantage which may not be reached under private property, while as respects the managing heads it is at a considerable disadvantage." [1]

Again in regard to the apportionment of labour between occupations, there is a marked change of emphasis. In the later editions of the *Principles* the difficulties had been acknowledged, but it had been hoped that they would not be " insuperable ". Now they are difficulties inherent in the system. " The arrangement, therefore, which is deemed indispensable to a just distribution would probably be a very considerable disadvantage in respect of production." Moreover, it is to be feared that it would give rise to political difficulties. " It is probable that a Communist association would frequently fail to exhibit the attractive

[1] *Fortnightly Review*, vol. xxv, New Series (1879), p. 520.

picture of mutual love and unity of will and feeling which we are often told by Communists to expect, but would often be torn by dissension and not infrequently broken up by it."

Finally, the danger to liberty is stated much more strongly than before. Under communism " there would be less scope for the development of individual character and individual preference than has hitherto existed among the full citizens of any state belonging to the progressive branches of the human family. Already in all societies the compression of individuality by the majority is a great and growing evil ; it would probably be much greater under Communism, except so far as it might be in the power of individuals to set bounds to it by selecting to belong to a community of persons like-minded with themselves."

In spite of this, Mill goes on, very characteristically, to add that he does " not seek to draw any inference against the possibility that Communistic production is capable of being at some future time the form of society best adapted to the wants and circumstances of mankind ". This will long be an open question. " The one certainty is, that Communism to be successful, requires a high standard of both moral and intellectual education in all members of the community." Mill thinks that progress to such a condition must necessarily be slow and urges those who believe in communism to demonstrate the validity of their hopes by voluntary experiments. If they can show that they can be successful, well and good. " But to force unprepared populations into Communist societies, even if a political revolution gave the power to make the attempt, would end in disappointment." [1]

---

[1] There follows at this point a digression on the possibilities of Fourierism. This system always had for Mill the special merit of starting from a recognition

All this, it must be remembered, is concerned with small communistic groups on the scale of the village or township. When he comes to deal with " the more ambitious plan which aims at taking possession of the whole land and capital of the country, and beginning at once to administer it on the public account ", Mill is much more decided. " The very idea of conducting the whole industry of a country by direction from a single centre is so obviously chimerical that nobody ventures to propose any mode in which it should be done. . . . The problem of management, which we have seen to be so difficult even to a select population well prepared beforehand, would be thrown down to be solved as best it could by aggregations united only by locality or taken indiscriminately from the population, including all the malefactors. . . . It is saying but little to say that the introduction of socialism under such conditions could have no effect but disastrous failure, and its apostles could have only the consolation that the order of society as it now exists would have perished first, and all who

of what he regarded as one of the main problems of pure Communism, the difficulty of making labour attractive ; he was fascinated by the ingenuity shown by Fourier and his followers in trying to get round this difficulty. His opinions on its practicability seem to have undergone something of the mysterious vicissitudes characteristic of his opinions on socialism in general. In the second edition of the *Principles*, where it first makes its appearance, after praising its ingenuity, he dwells on what he describes as " the unmanageable nature of its machinery ". In the third edition, the eulogies are maintained but the strictures are omitted and a plea is made for a practical experiment. In the chapters under present discussion, there is no renewal of the main strictures ; but the presentation is more detached : the reference is continually to the claims and expectations of its proponents and the emphasis is more than ever on the desirability of " that fair trial which alone can test the workableness of any new scheme of social life " (*op. cit.* p. 524). I cannot think that it is wholly irrelevant that in a footnote recommending the writings of Fourier, the reader is warned that together with " unmistakable proofs of genius " he will find " the wildest and most unscientific fancies respecting the physical world and much interesting but rash speculation on the past and future history of humanity ". It is difficult not to suspect that between 1852 and 1869 Mill may have discovered something of the truth relating to this most peculiar and eccentric personality.

benefit by it would be involved in the common ruin —
a consolation which to some of them would probably be
real for, if appearances can be trusted, the animating
principle of too many of the revolutionary socialists is
hate ; a very excusable hatred of existing evils, which
would vent itself by putting an end to the present
system at all costs even to those who suffer by it, in
the hope that out of chaos would arise a better Kosmos,
and in the impatience of desperation respecting any
more gradual improvement. They are unaware that
chaos is the very most unfavourable position for setting
out in the construction of a Kosmos, and that many ages
of conflict, violence and tyrannical oppression of the
weak by the strong must intervene." [1]

(vi) *Interpretation of the Variations*

What are we to make of all this ? The arguments and
the position are clear enough. But the degree of continuity with Mill's earlier thought is perhaps in doubt.
To what extent are we here confronted with yet another
change of front ? To what extent are we to regard
these last papers as embodying a retractation of the
position of the later editions of the *Principles* ?

So far as revolutionary socialism is conceived, the
position is unambiguous. Mill had not dealt with this at
any length before ; and, had he done so, I do not think
the result would have been in doubt. The conception
of discontinuous change on a large scale, with its danger
to individual happiness and liberty, was so alien to his
whole attitude of mind, that I cannot believe that there
was ever a time when he would not have condemned it

---

[1] On Mill's attitude to the First International, see a letter to G. Brandes
Letters of John Stuart Mill (edited Hugh Elliot), vol. ii, p. 335.

as vigorously as he did in the passages which I have just quoted.

But what about the more limited projects — the " duodecimo editions of the New Jerusalem ", as the *Communist Manifesto* called them ?   Here it is hard to deny a certain change of view, a partial reversion, as Ashley suggested,[1] to the mood in which the first edition of the *Principles* was written.

The more closely the actual wording of the arguments is compared, the more difficult it is to avoid this conclusion.   An outsider, knowing nothing of Mill's history and background, would certainly say, " this man has moved to a more sceptical position ".

Nevertheless I suspect that it is possible to exaggerate this contrast, not so much by emphasis on the scepticism of the *Chapters on Socialism* as by too positive an interpretation of the original changes in the *Principles*. It must be remembered that in the chapter on Property, Mill never said that the type of socialism he was discussing was ultimately workable or desirable ; he said that it was an open question and that we had not yet the information which would enable us to judge.   When, in the chapter *On the Probable Future of the Labouring Classes*, he did express a view as to the probable direction of progress and the ultimately desirable goal, it related to an essentially vague ascent *via* co-partnership to some kind of co-operative productive association more syndicalist than socialist in conception.   If we couple with this the fact that even in the chapter on *Property* he dwelt as strongly on the possibilities of change in the property system itself as on any possibilities of socialism, and if we remember the earnestness with which again and again he returned to this theme, it is difficult to believe that the changes in the section on communism

---

[1] See his edition of Mill's *Principles*, Appendix K.

were intended to go much further than a plea for an open mind, or that his willingness to be designated socialist meant much more than a willingness to be classified as one who regarded all existing institutions as " provisional " and a disinclination to be classified with those who regarded the argument as closed.

This interpretation, I suggest, is strongly supported by his correspondence. There is a letter to a Mr. Jay of New York,[1] in which he protests strongly against the praise which he had received in an article in the *North American Review*. The writer, he says, " is one whose tone of thinking and feeling is extremely repugnant to me. He gives a totally false idea of the book and of its author when he makes me a participant in the derision with which he speaks of Socialists of all kinds and degrees." Temperamentally, Mill was always prepared to go to hell with those whom he regarded as intellectuals rather than to heaven with those whom he regarded as philistines — even if he was not quite sure that the intellectuals were right. Hence it jarred on him that what he said in the first edition should be over-simplified and quoted by the sort of people towards whom he felt the greatest antipathy ; to find himself in the same boat with the smug and complacent who had no idea of the provisionality of all social institutions and who confused him with the vulgarizers [2] of the earlier Classical system, was an intensely distasteful experience. When he came to prepare a new edition, therefore, his treatment and his willingness to enlarge his view of the possibilities were conditioned at least in part by his determination to leave no further room for this kind of association. That in making his revisions he stated the case in a way in

---

[1] *Letters of J. S. Mill* (edited Hugh Elliot), vol. i, pp. 138-139.

[2] One of the few conceited remarks to be found in the whole range of Mill's writings is where he reproaches Kingsley for coupling his name " with that of a mere tyro like Harriet Martineau ". *Ibid.* p. 157.

which he was not willing to restate it later on, seems to me to be certain. The differences between the treatment in later editions of the *Principles* and in the *Posthumous Chapters* are unmistakable. But overstatement was not unusual with Mill. As I urged at the beginning, apparently the most purely intellectual, in fact he was one of the most emotional of writers. This, of course, was one of the sources of his power. But it was also an occasional source of inconsistency, especially through time, as moods changed; and if I am not mistaken, it was the main, though probably not the only, reason for the apparent inconsistency here.[1]

---

[1] Whatever be our conclusions regarding this difficult matter, nothing can be more certain than Mill's attitude to nationalization as conceived in our own day. In his *Liberty*, the work of which he expected the greatest lasting value, he expressed himself as follows :

" If the roads, the railways, the banks, the insurance offices, the great joint-stock companies, the universities, and the public charities, were all of them branches of the government ; if, in addition, the municipal corporations and local boards, with all that now devolves on them, became departments of the central administration ; if the employees of all these different enterprises were appointed and paid by the government, and looked to the government for every rise in life ; not all the freedom of the press and popular constitution of the legislature would make this or any other country free otherwise than in name. And the evil would be greater, the more efficiently and scientifically the administrative machinery was constructed — the more skilful the arrangements for obtaining the best qualified hands and heads with which to work it." (*Op. cit.*, 1st edition, 1859, pp. 198–9.)

THE CLASSICAL THEORY IN GENERAL PERSPECTIVE

(i) *Introduction*

WE are now nearing the end of our journey. We have surveyed the System of Economic Freedom as presented by the English Classical Economists, their theory of the economic functions of the state, their contribution to the solution of the problem of the condition of the people and their attitude to collectivist notions ; and although there are matters which we have not dealt with extensively, such as their views on external economic policy and special problems of public finance, these may be regarded as matters of detail which to dwell on at length in this context would distort the proportions of our treatment. But, before bringing the inquiry to a close, it does seem worth while to stand still further back, so to speak, and to try to get a general picture of the Classical theory of policy as a whole. What does it look like in the large ? What is its general significance in the broad perspective of the history of social philosophy ?

(ii) *The Classical Economists as Reformers*

The first thing we have to note when trying to get this general view is that the Classical Economists were reformers and that the theory of economic policy in

English Classical political economy was a theory of economic and social reform. I use the words reform and reformers, not with the intention of conveying any special penumbra of approbation, but simply to designate an historic role and a psychological attitude. The Classical Economists were not revolutionaries, no Classical Economist ever advocated the violent overthrow of governments or the total abolition of the historic basis of society. But they were critics of some contemporary institutions and some contemporary habits, and they had definite proposals for what they deemed to be improvement, which they advocated with more or less energy.

Now it is important not to over-simplify — even when trying to establish broad views. The lives of the men whom we have designated as Classical Economists cover a stretch of a hundred and fifty years, if we measure from the birth of David Hume to the death of John Stuart Mill — years during which conditions in this island changed from those of a mainly rural and mercantile community, governed chiefly by a landowning aristocracy, to those of a predominantly urban and manufacturing community, tending towards pure democracy. It is not to be expected that the pace or the extent of proposals for reform should be the same at the beginning of the period as they became later on. Furthermore, we have to take account of differences of temperament. It is a far cry from the detachment of a David Hume to the zeal of a John Stuart Mill, and a man would be insensitive indeed who attributed to Senior and McCulloch the same texture of character or outlook.

Nevertheless there can be no doubt that, in the broad sweep of history, the English Classical School from its beginnings in the philosophic speculations of Hume and Smith down to the very practical preoccupations of Senior and the Benthamites, must be regarded in its attitude to policy as a school of economic and social reform. It was not merely this ; for its exponents were not concerned only with policy but also with the very foundations of economic science — which are something quite different from a theory of policy. But that it was a reform movement and that the Classical Economists are to be classified, in this aspect, as reformers, is a proposition which, although it is often forgotten, should not be open to serious question.

(iii) *The Theory of Policy and Political Economy*

But this description does not carry us very far. The history of the last three hundred years in this country has to take note of many reform movements and many schools of reformers. What distinguishes the Classical Theory of Economic Policy from most of these is that, rightly or wrongly, it professed to be based upon a systematic body of scientific knowledge — the newly emerging science of political economy. The prescriptions which it laid down were supposed to derive, in part at least, from a systematic inquiry into the nature of economic relationships and their mode of development in different types of circumstances. This was true equally of the general prescriptions of the System of Economic Freedom or of the detailed maxims of the Ricardian theory of taxation.

It is important to be clear about the precise nature of this characteristic. Quite obviously it does not consist in the mere fact that, in the framing of practical prescriptions, some regard was had to their probable consequences. Few theories of policy, save those said to be based directly upon the explicit pronouncements of some deity, have been able entirely to dispense with this. Certainly, in the sphere of economic policy, the literature of earlier times abounds with investigations of the probable consequences of particular measures. What distinguishes the Classical theory from all this is, not that it paid some regard to consequences before making recommendations, but rather that its regard to consequences was based upon a more or less comprehensive analysis of the economic system as a whole. In France, in the hands of Cantillon and the Physiocrats, and in Britain, in the hands of the Scotch Philosophers, economics had passed from a series of *ad hoc* inquiries to an analysis of general interconnexions.[1] It appealed to general uniformities rather than particular instances. It presented principles of explanation applicable to a wide variety of circumstances. In short, it had assumed the form and the objectives of a science in the Kantian sense. It was on this body of knowledge, at least in part, that the English Classical Economists professed to base their theory of policy. And it is this claim which is one of the chief characteristics distinguishing them from most other schools.

Of course, this claim may be questioned. Extremes meet ; and in the works, both of the Marxians and of members of the German Historical School, it is not unusual to encounter the suggestion that the scientific basis of the Classical theory was just a façade. The Classical Economists and the others, it is argued, were equally concerned with certain practical objectives. The appeal to an objective body of knowledge was essentially a blind, an extremely ingenious supporting argument, rigged after the conclusions to be established had been

---

[1] The change is nowhere better described than in the relevant chapter of Schumpeter's *Epochen des Dogmen- und Methodengeschichte*, which bears the appropriate title : " Die Entdeckung des wirtschaftlichen Kreislaufs ".

reached by an entirely different process. First, the policy to be recommended ; then the apparatus of scientific justification : that, according to this view, was the actual psychological sequence.

Now, I am not here concerned to vindicate the objective validity of the system of Classical analysis. Who, indeed, after a hundred years' further development, would wish to contend that it had attained final truth or that parts of it were not marked by extreme inadequacy and, at times, by positive error ? But I am concerned with the origins of the Classical theory of policy. And I am bound to say that, on due consideration of the evidence, I find this type of explanation highly unconvincing. Of course here too we must not over-simplify. There can be no doubt that the stimulus to much of the abstract analysis came from interest in practical problems : Ricardo's interest in value and distribution was evoked by his interest in the corn laws. It is common ground that the history of thought is not to be pursued in a vacuum ; the idea of a complete well-rounded system of economic analysis springing from the heads of Smith, Quesnay and Ricardo, independent of its historical setting and the stimuli of practical interest is, of course, entirely fanciful, if indeed it has ever been presented save as a dummy for destructive criticism. But the occasion for thought is one thing ; its working out and the logical tests to which the results are submitted are something entirely different. I do not believe that an unprejudiced reading of the works of the Classical authors can lead to any conclusion but that the scientific part of these works, however evoked and however liable to error and occasional bias, was something which had a status and a momentum of its own, subject to the general tests of scientific inquiry and acquiring, as time went on, a coherence and force which gave it, as it were, independent authority when they turned to considerations of policy. It would be tedious, in this context, to argue this matter at length. But if there be any of you, not committed to the dogmas of a party line who have yet some doubts on the subject, read Hume on money, Smith on the division of labour and the market, or Mill on the equation of international demand, as he called it, and ask yourselves whether there is not there the texture and the substance of genuine scientific inquiry — whatever you may think of the finality or the comprehensiveness of the results.

If it were otherwise — and if it were, we, as well as they, would be involved — the deception was very deep down, far below the level at which the introspective eye can discover self-deception. For, unless these people were engaged in deliberate lying on a scale which it would be very difficult to organize and still more difficult to carry through without self-betrayal, there can be no doubt that they thought that the science which they were in process of discovering was of immense value in forming the basis for an art of policy. You can see this in so sceptical a writer as Hume.[1] The same conviction is the basis of wide claims in the *Wealth of Nations*. The later Classical writers are quite explicit about it. A new science has been discovered. A knowledge of its laws must henceforward be indispensable to legislators.[2] One of the main hopes of human improvement is the diffusion of a wide knowledge of its principles.[3]

---

[1] *Essays* (edited Green and Grose), vol. i, p. 99. " So great is the force of laws, and of particular forms of government, and so little dependence have they on the humours and tempers of men, that consequences almost as general may sometimes be deduced from them, as any which the mathematical sciences afford us." The particular reference is to politics. But there can be no doubt of its wider applicability in this part of Hume's system.

[2] McCulloch, *A Discourse on the Rise, Progress, Peculiar Objects and Importance of Political Economy* (2nd edition), pp. 81, 82.

[3] Senior, *An Introductory Lecture on Political Economy*, especially pp. 21-24. See also Ricardo, *Letters to Trower*, p. 163.

Perhaps the most striking declaration of this belief, although it has attracted very little attention, is to be found in a dialogue by James Mill entitled *Whether Political Economy is Useful*.[1] In this curious production, the most austere of the Benthamites, writing in the year of his death, reaches what, for him, were most unusual heights of eloquence concerning the utility of political economy. It is valuable in itself, he claims, as providing the pleasures of understanding highly intricate trains of events " as a man raising himself to an eminence from which he can look down upon a scene of the highest possible interest, not only beholds the numerous objects of which it consists, and their visible motions, but the causes of them and the ends to which they are directed, and thence derives the highest delight ". But it is further essential to the proper ordering of society.

B. " We may then, I think, lay it down, with your consent, as a general proposition, that wherever a great many agents and operations are combined for the production of a certain result, or set of results, a commanding view of the whole is absolutely necessary for effecting that combination in the most perfect manner."

A. " I agree."

B. " But a commanding view of a whole subject, in all its parts, and the connexion of those parts, is it anything but another name for the theory, or science of the subject. Theory ($\theta\epsilon\omega\rho\iota\alpha$) is literally VIEW : and science is *scientia*, KNOWLEDGE ; meaning view, or knowledge, not solely of this and that part but, like that of the general with his army, of the *whole*."

A. " I see the inference to which you are proceeding :

---

[1] *London Review*, vol. ii, July/January 1835–36, pp. 553-571. The attribution is by Bain. See his *James Mill : A Biography*, p. 403.

you mean to say, that the theory or science of political economy is a commanding view of the vast combination of agents and operations engaged in producing for the use of man, the whole of the things which he enjoys and consumes : in other words, the things which he denominates the matter of wealth — the great object to which almost all the toils and cares of human beings are directed."

B. " You have anticipated me correctly."

A. " You would farther proceed to ask me, I have no doubt, whether the innumerable operations which take place in subservience to that end, may not take place in more ways than one ; in short, in a worse way, or a better way ? Whether it is not of importance that they should take place in the best way ? And whether the difference between the best way and the worst way is not likely to be very great. . . . And to all these questions I should answer in the affirmative." [1]

(iv) *The Theory of Policy and the Principle of Utility*

I hope I have now said enough to demonstrate to you the sense of power and direction which was given to the Classical Theory of Policy by the possession of what was thought to be a comprehensive body of economic analysis. With the exception of Physiocracy, it was the first reform movement which based its prescriptions on explicit appeal to this sort of knowledge.

But economic analysis was not the only basis of this theory. Indeed it was in the nature of things that there must be something else. For you cannot build

---

[1] It is perhaps not unnatural that, after eliciting so satisfactory a response, the triumphant B should go on to say, " I should become in love with controversy, if I always met with such controversialists as you ".

prescriptions on a mere knowledge of positive facts, however systematized and comprehensive. You need a goal as well — a general objective, a criterion of the expected results of action. It is all very well to know how the world works, why certain relations emerge in certain conditions, how these relations change when conditions are altered. But unless you have some test whereby you can distinguish good from bad, desirable consequences from undesirable, you are without an essential constituent of a theory of policy. You are like the captain of a ship equipped with charts and compasses and all the means of propulsion and steering, but without an assigned destination. A theory of economic policy, in the sense of a body of precepts for action, must take its ultimate criterion from outside economics.

This criterion the English Classical Economists found in the principle of utility, the principle that the test of policy is to be its effect on human happiness. All action, all laws and institutions were to be judged by this test. If their consequences were such as promote more happiness (or eliminate more unhappiness) than was conceivable from other actions, laws or institutions, they were good ; if not, then they were bad.

This attitude is common to all the English Classical Economists. We get the picture badly out of focus if we conceive that reliance on the principle of utility was confined to Bentham and his immediate circle. It is, of course, undeniable that the greatest happiness principle owes its sharpest formulation and its most explicit and continuous use to Bentham and his followers. But utilitarianism as an ethical theory and appeal to the principle of utility as a criterion of social arrangements did not originate with Bentham. If we are to single out any one name for the credit (or discredit) of having first formulated it as the basis of a fully developed system of social philosophy, it must be Hume rather than Bentham : and there is much to be said for the view that, until we come to Sidgwick, it is the Humean, rather than the Benthamite, formulation, which is the more persuasive and generally plausible. Certainly it is in the Humean rather than the Benthamite sense that we may claim to label the entire Classical School as utilitarian in outlook. The only possible exception is Adam Smith, who had a moral philosophy of his own which in some respects appears to be in contrast with the utilitarian outlook. But here, as so often, Smith's apparent principles are belied by his practice. Whatever the nature of the *Theory of Moral Sentiments*, the tests of policy applied throughout the entire *Wealth of Nations* are, in fact, consistently utilitarian in substance.

In adopting this attitude, it is clear that the Classical Economists placed themselves in a position of sharp contrast with all those thinkers who base their prescriptions for policy on ethical systems assigning absolute value to certain institutions or types of conduct — systems of natural rights, natural law, theological systems involving the sacrosanctity of particular institutions. On the utilitarian view no institutions, no systems of rights, were sacrosanct. All were subject to the test of utility. The famous Chapter II in the *Principles of Morals and Legislation* makes this opposition perfectly explicit.

Nevertheless, it would be a mistake to interpret the principle of utility as implying no element of lasting value in institutions, no principles of morals involving more than a calculus of immediate pleasure and pain. It was perfectly consistent with this principle to attach, as indeed there was attached, the greatest value to stable institutions and general rules of conduct. The greatest happiness was not the greatest happiness at the moment, but the greatest happiness over time; and, on the basis of this principle, the most powerful arguments could be deployed in favour of security of expectation and consistency in behaviour, which in turn afforded strong grounds for more or less settled codes of law and morals. On the utilitarian outlook, social arrangements were not provisional in the sense that they were liable to day-to-day change and upset; they were provisional only in the sense that they were all liable to the ultimate test of their ability to promote human happiness.

It is no business of mine in these lectures to investigate the validity of this principle. My business here, as elsewhere, is to try to set out what the Classical Economists said and what were the assumptions underlying their attitude — to explain, not to evaluate. Nevertheless, before passing on, it may be worth while disposing of one or two criticisms arising in this connexion which rest obviously on misconception; this, not with a view to any ultimate judgment, but rather with a view to bringing out more clearly the real import of their attitude.

In the first place, it may be well to note that the conventional nature of the utilitarian assumption did not escape notice. It is a fundamental difficulty of utilitarian ethics that it appears to involve the comparability and summation of the satisfactions of different individuals. If this were indeed possible in any direct manner, then the only normative element in any utilitarian prescription would be the proposition that happiness ought to be maximized. The best would be a question of measurement and calculation. But, in fact, it is not possible; and the weighting which is given to the satisfactions of different individuals is another element which partakes of the nature of an ethical postulate rather than a principle established by observation or introspection. Among the English utilitarians the assumption was that each man's capacity for happiness was to be counted as equal. But it is easily possible to think of other assumptions which might be held to be equally binding ; I have elsewhere quoted the example of Sir Henry Maine's Indian Brahmin who held that, " according to the clear teaching of his religion, a Brahmin was entitled to twenty times as much happiness as anybody else ".[1]

Now, whatever may have been the case in modern times, this problem did not escape attention in the Classical period. Among the Bentham manuscripts at University College, Halévy discovered a very remarkable fragment entitled " Dimension of Happiness " which makes this very clear. " 'Tis in vain ", says Bentham, " to talk of adding quantities which after the addition will continue distinct as they were before, one man's happiness will never be another man's happiness : a gain to one man is no gain to another : you might as well pretend to add twenty apples to twenty pears, which after you had done that would not be forty of any one thing but twenty of each just as there were before. . . . This addibility of the happiness of different subjects, however, when considered rigorously, it may appear fictitious, is a *postulatum* [my italics] without the allowance of which all practical reasoning is at a stand. . . ."[2] Maine was therefore fully justified when he suggested that the doctrine that " one shall only count as one " was for Bentham " nothing more than a working rule of legislation ".[3]

---

[1] See Maine's *Early History of Institutions*, p. 399. See also a note by me on " Interpersonal Comparisons of Utility ", *Economic Journal*, December 1938.

[2] Halévy, *Growth of Philosophical Radicalism*, p. 495. Bentham goes on to suggest that the postulate is on the same footing as " the equality of chances to reality on which the whole branch of Mathematics which is called the doctrine of chances is established ".   [3] Maine, *op. cit.* p. 399.

Furthermore, we may note that this working rule was never actually made to bear the quantitative implications which have sometimes been read into it. There is much talk in the Benthamite literature of a felicific calculus ; and the term naturally suggests a most pretentious apparatus of measurement and computation. But, in fact, this is all shop window. The mathematical exposition of such a calculus, its equations of second differentials and the like, with the implication that, given sufficient statistics, there exists here a guide to legislators, is something which comes much later. There is no need to investigate the question whether this would have seemed as quaint to Bentham and his friends as it does to some of us. The fact is that their use of the felicific calculus lay in quite another direction — in rough judgments of the expediency of particular items of the penal law, in general estimates of the suitability of existing institutions or the desirability of other institutions to take their place. It was not necessary for all this that they should have used such a pretentious label ; and it is to be noted that David Hume, whose procedure was essentially similar, never indulged in such flourishes. But if we are to form correct views, it is by what they did, rather than by what might be read into their terminology, that they must be judged : and there can be no doubt that their practice was in the sphere of broad appraisals rather than quantitative computations.

(v) *Individualism as an End*

To understand correctly the ethical presuppositions of the Classical theory, it is important not to rest content with the mere identification of their utilitarianism. They were indeed utilitarians ; but they were more than this :

they were individualist utilitarians. The greatest happiness which they sought was not a happiness which was, so to speak, imposed from outside ; it was a happiness which was to be judged by the individuals concerned. This is a matter which demands some further attention, for it is certainly not logically implicit in what has already been said; nor is it certain that it is a position which, without further elaboration, is completely logically coherent.

It should be reasonably clear that there is nothing in utilitarianism as such which implies an individualistic norm. If it be assumed that the majority of the citizens are ignorant and stupid — for which it would not be difficult to collect some evidence in experience — and if it be assumed that rulers are enlightened and unselfish — which might be harder to sustain empirically — there is nothing in the principle of utility which would preclude the inference that the greatest happiness was to be found in a state in which the goals of production and development were set, not by the choice of the citizens, but by the choice of some central bureau. It is indeed unlikely that such an arrangement would have commended itself to many of those who, in some form or other, have accepted utilitarian or eudaemonistic tests ; only Plato and the modern dictators have wished to push people around quite as much as this. But it is probable that the majority view in this tradition would involve some degree of paternalism : and it is almost certain that this is the implicit assumption of normal lay reactions. An emphasis on individual choice as the final criterion of happiness — individualism as a goal — is something quite exceptional in the history of social philosophy.

But it was a very definite feature of the Classical theory ; we do not conceive that theory correctly unless we recognize the essential role played in it by the individualist norm.

What exactly does this involve ?

It should be quite clear, in the first place, that it does *not* involve a denial of the existence and the necessity of some means of meeting what may be called communal needs. In the first lecture, when I was outlining the main features of the so-called system of economic freedom, I was at pains to draw your attention to the universal recognition in the Classical literature of the importance of the needs, such as defence, street lighting and sanitation, which can only be met by arrangements involving indiscriminate benefit. There cannot be any doubt about the Classical attitude here. All that needs emphasis perhaps is the part which it played in enlarging conceptions of the scope of this kind of need.

In the second place, it should be also quite clear that it did not involve denial of the utility of paternalism in the case of children and backward peoples. The Classical Economists were among the first to point out the absurdity, the inhumanity, of the assumption that children of tender years should be treated as if they were adults in the matter of freedom of choice of occupation or responsibility for their own education. As for the special problem of backward peoples, it must never be forgotten that the two Mills, who were in many respects the most radical of all the Classical Economists in their emphasis on the individualist norm, were also officials of the East India Company and were well acquainted with the special responsibilities of government in areas where the great body of the people could not by any stretch of imagination be conceived as being capable of being guided for their own good by reason and persuasion.[1] I have already quoted a passage from John

---

[1] It would be a study well worth making, on the basis of Mill's dispatches and papers on behalf of the East India Company, to attempt to get into systematic order his opinions in this respect.

Stuart Mill, in which he contends that, in such cases, there is nothing which it may not be desirable or even necessary for government to do : and although this passage related overtly to the organization of means rather than the setting of ultimate ends, I have no doubt that it would be quite consistent with its underlying spirit to read this extension into it. I know no reason to suppose that any other Classical Economist would have adopted any other attitude.

But — and this is the vital, the significant difference — although the Classical Economists were no less aware than the exponents of avowedly authoritarian systems of the occasional necessity for paternalism, they differed from others in this respect in that they emphasized continually the desirability of getting away from it. Although at certain times and at certain places it might be necessary to recognize the ignorance and incapacity of the people to understand what is good for them, it was always their aim to bring it about that such conditions ceased to exist. Paternalism might from time to time be necessary as a safeguard against even more intolerable evils. But it was only in a society of individuals, free so far as technical conditions permitted to shape their own ends, that positive good was permanently realizable.

This attitude, as I have said, was general. But the justification thereof varied. I have quoted to you Bentham's argument for freedom of choice in consumption : the absence of freedom involves constraint which in itself is painful ; moreover, the governments which, in fact, people are likely to get are not so likely to know the interest of the individual as the individual himself. Doubtless this is the basic attitude. The Classical Economists as a group had a poor opinion of the wisdom of governments and a strong suspicion that, in fact, it was likely to prove the vehicle of special interests. Even

when they gave formal acknowledgment of the possibility of a beneficial paternalism, they were apt to
regard it as a somewhat improbable accident. As John
Stuart Mill put it, if people were not capable of being
guided by reason and persuasion then, perhaps, a
benevolent despot, an Akbar, was an advantage.[1] But
there was always a strong penumbra of assumption that
Akbars were rare occurrences in human history. I am
clear that this was the typical attitude.

When we come to John Stuart Mill, however, the
emphasis varies. As we have seen already, although the
extent of his support is capable of exaggeration, Mill was
much more willing than any of his predecessors to
sympathize with experiment in collectivist *organization*.
It is all the more interesting and significant therefore,
that he was even more opposed to collectivist *choice*. If
you read Bentham carefully you will occasionally find
passages, especially in his early work, in which it would
seem that, for the moment, he attached more importance
to good government than to free government. On a
balanced view, I am sure that to emphasize such *obiter
dicta* would be an error of perspective. But there is no
doubt that they exist; nor is there any doubt at all
of the paramountcy in his mind of the principle of
utility : for him the individualistic norm in the sphere
of ends, is clearly in the nature of a corollary. But with
Mill, especially in his later phases, this was certainly
not true. For the author of *Liberty*, it was obviously
much more important that choice should be free than
that it should be good. It is true that his defence of
freedom is on utilitarian lines : it is of fundamental

---

[1] " Liberty, as a principle, has no application to any state of things anterior
to the time when mankind have become capable of being improved by free
and equal discussion. Until then there is nothing for them but implicit obedience
to an Akbar or a Charlemagne, if they are so fortunate as to find one " (*Liberty*
(Blackwell reprint), p. 9).

importance to society that opinions, whether true or false, should be freely ventilated ; for who can tell in advance which is true and which is false ? But here, as elsewhere, it is difficult to read Mill on social philosophy without feeling that insensibly he had reached a position which, in fact, involved a plurality of ultimate criteria. The maxim that good government was no substitute for free government is, of course, capable, on certain assumptions, of being reconciled with a purely utilitarian outlook. But on other assumptions, this is not quite so certain. Yet there is no doubt where Mill's convictions permanently lay.

But be this as it may — a difficult matter involving problems of moral and social philosophy which are possibly still unsettled — we do no harm by considering the individualism of the Classical Economists in the sphere of ends as something which at any rate for most practical purposes stands, so to speak, on its own legs. Whether, in the last analysis, it was derived from certain applications of the utilitarian calculus or whether it had independent and autonomous standing is perhaps an open question. But it is not an open question that to understand their attitude in the realm of ends we must regard the Classical Economists as being both utilitarians and individualists in this sense.

(vi) *Individualism as a Means : the System of Economic Freedom once again*

Now it is quite possible to be an individualist utilitarian as regards ends and yet to be something quite other than individualist as regards means. We know indeed that some of the finest minds that have given their support to the idea of a collectivist organization of production have yet been pure individualists and utilitarians in their formulation of the aims of society. To some of us it may seem odd that a school of thought which has laid such emphasis, such undue emphasis perhaps, on the influence on culture of technique and organization, should be able to believe that, in a state of affairs in which society owns all and the individual nothing, the individual should yet be freer and more at liberty to shape his ends than in a society in which some at least of the means of production and new initiative are the property of private individuals. But it is a matter of historical record that to successive generations of the Left in Western European politics, there has seemed nothing contradictory in such a position.

It was not so with the Classical Economists. They were both individualists as regards ends and (with due reservations) individualists as regards means. For them, an organization of production, based, in the main, on private property and the market, was an essential complement to a system of freedom of choice as regards consumption and provision for the future. They believed that, within an appropriate framework of law, such an organization could be made to work harmoniously. They believed that it would work better than alternative practicable systems. They, therefore, believed it to be justified on utilitarian and individualist criteria. Even John Stuart Mill, who, as we have seen, was very willing to experiment with limited local collectivism, was a whole-hearted believer in competition and the competitive market.

I hope that I have emphasized this sufficiently. These lectures have been concerned with the theory of policy of the English Classical Economists ; and for that reason, and because it has been necessary to clear away certain absurd misconceptions, it has been necessary to devote much time and space to their theory of positive state action — to the *agenda* of the state as distinct from the *sponte acta* of individuals, to revert to Bentham's phraseology. But from the outset I have urged upon you that the conception of a decentralized organization of production resting on private property and the market was central to their whole position. I risked dullness in my first lecture by putting this in the foreground of my exposition.

But I hope too that, having emphasized this, I have also succeeded in making it clear that this is only one part of the picture : that, in order that the individualistic organization of production might work satisfactorily, there was also postulated a whole complex of necessary functions of government. Whatever may have been the view of other schools of thought, the philosophical anarchists or the liberals of the *Naturrecht*, the English Classical Economists never conceived the system of economic freedom as arising *in vacuo* or functioning in a system of law and order so simple and so minimal as to be capable of being written down on a limited table of stone (or a revolutionary handbill) and restricted to the functions of the night watchman. Nothing less than the whole complex of the Benthamite codes — Civil, Penal and Constitutional — was an adequate framework for their system.

Let us try to recall in essence what this broad conception was.

We may remind ourselves in the first place that it embraced the whole sphere of activities affording indiscriminate benefit. Not, of course, that it implied that each and every possible kind of indiscriminate benefit should actually be provided ; that was a matter for weighing in some rough-and-ready manner the benefits thus obtained against the benefits which would be withdrawn from the discriminate benefit sector if scarce resources were used for this purpose. But the formal principle was assumed; and, as regards its substantial realization, it is perhaps worth noting that the recommendations of the Classical Economists often went much further than those of their predecessors. Certainly it is a piquant fact, usually overlooked by the historians of thought, that as regards the organization of this kind of service these recommendations were much more *étatiste* than the *status quo*: it was the Classical Economists who were among the leaders of the movement for making private monopolies public property in this respect. There was no use for private armies, private police, private highways in their system; in this respect they were far less *laissez-faire* than the Mercantilists.

In the second place, we may recall that wide range of activities which may be grouped under the headings of the educative and the eleemosynary functions. I have no desire here to recapitulate in detail the various prescriptions in that respect which I discussed in the lecture on The Condition of the People. But it may perhaps be worth pointing out that the accusation that, in its practical prescriptions, political economy is apt to assume a population of adult males and females, to the neglect of the large element in any real population which consists of young children, invalids and helpless old people, has no grounds in the prescriptions of Classical Political Economy. The policies which they embodied may have been right or they may have been wrong — to investigate this is no part of my intention — but it cannot be contended that the problems were not recognized or that determined efforts were not made to provide solutions. The functions of the state as a supplement to the family find extensive recognition in the Classical theory of policy.

But beyond all this and far transcending it in importance in relation to the understanding of the System of Economic Freedom, was the provision of a set of rules which so limited and guided individual initiative, that the residue of free action undirected from the centre could be conceived to harmonize with the general objects of public interest. We get the System of Economic Freedom all wrong if we do not realize that it was only on the assumption of such a suitable framework of law and order that it was ever recommended by the group of men whose theories we are examining. Indeed, in any logical scheme, we must regard the provision of such a framework as *prior* to the recommendation of economic freedom. Historically, perhaps, from time to time the emphasis may have been different. Some framework of law and order, even if very defective, was part of the heritage of the past ; there were doubtless times when the elimination of absurd laws and regulations seemed a more important recommendation than the necessity of some law and some regulation at all times. But it is to betray a total absence of acquaintance with the literature to suppose that the prior necessity of the framework would ever have been called in question.

At this point it is perhaps desirable to examine for a moment a misunderstanding of a much more plausible, much more sophisticated nature. It arises in the work of Élie Halévy, perhaps the most eminent of all historians who have devoted their attention to the history of this school of thought. Now, of course, Halévy, the biographer of the philosophical radicals, was the last man in the world to ignore their positive contribution to the theory of law. Yet it was his contention that there was an inner contradiction in their system in that, while assuming that in the legal field it was the function of the legislator to bring about an artificial harmonization of interest, they assumed that in the economic field the harmony arose spontaneously.[1] This contention has had great influence. As Professor Viner has pointed out,[2] it has been taken over more or less uncritically by a whole succession of lesser writers and at the present day it has become, as it were, the small change of the books about books.

Now Halévy was a true *clerc* and a great man, not to be mentioned in the same breath with the other critics to whom I have had occasion to make allusion. But I find it difficult to believe that, in this respect, he was not mistaken. I see no evidence whatever for the view that the Classical Economists ever made the distinction which he attributes to them. If they assumed anywhere a harmony, it was never a harmony arising in a vacuum but always very definitely within a framework of law. It is not true that the theory of property either in Hume or in Bentham was constructed without an eye to its economic implications. It is not true that their conception of contract was a conception of something outside the sphere of economic relationships. If no other proof were available, their complete willingness to apply special rules and regulations where, for technical reasons, competition was not possible, should be a sufficient indication of the extent to which they regarded the appropriate legal framework and the system of economic freedom as two aspects of one and the same social process.[3]

But, as a matter of fact, much more conclusive proof is actually available. For the question which is raised by Halévy's strictures, the question, namely, whether it

[1] See Halévy, *The Growth of Philosophical Radicalism*, especially pp. 498-499.
[2] " Bentham and J. S. Mill: the Utilitarian Background ", *American Economic Review*, vol. xxxix, No. 2, March 1949.
[3] On this point Professor W. H. Hutt has a very cogent footnote in his *Economists and the Public*, p. 136.

is possible to distinguish between the sphere of legal and economic relations in the way suggested, was, in fact, raised by Bentham himself and answered by a conclusive negative. In his *View of a Complete Code of Laws*, there is a chapter (Chapter XXVIII, " Of Political Economy "), of which the subject matter is a treatment of just this question. It is possible, Bentham argues, to distinguish political economy as a separate branch of the general science of legislation. But it is not so easy, he says, to say what laws are economical and what are not. As for a separate code of economic laws, the thing is an impossibility. " I do not see ", he says, " that there can exist a code of laws concerning political economy distinct and separate from all other codes. *The collection of laws upon this subject would only be a mass of imperfect shreds, drawn without distinction from the whole body of laws* " [1] (my italics). This is surely proof conclusive that Bentham would have rejected, as inherently self-contradictory, any idea of a distinction between an artificial harmony created by law and a spontaneous harmony created by economic behaviour. In so far as there was harmony at all, the harmony created by law was the harmony arising from behaviour within the framework of the law. There was no dualism in this respect, the conception was essentially one and indivisible.

Thus, if we dig right down to the foundations, what distinguishes the Classical outlook from the authoritarian systems is not a denial of the necessity for state action on the one side and an affirmation on the other, but rather a different view of what kind of action is desirable. The authoritarian wishes to issue from the centre, or at least from organs more or less directly controlled from the centre, positive instructions concerning what

[1] Bentham, *op. cit.* vol. iii, p. 203.

shall be done all along the line all the time. In contrast to this attitude, the Classical liberal does not say that the centre should do nothing. But, believing that the attempt to plan actual quantities from the centre is liable to break down and that no such plan can be a substitute for truly decentralized initiative, he proposes, as it were, a division of labour:[1] the state shall prescribe what individuals shall not do, if they are not to get in each other's way, while the citizens shall be left free to do anything which is not so forbidden. To the one is assigned the task of establishing formal rules, to the other responsibility for the substance of specific action.

This contrast can be put another way. For the Classical liberal, the characteristic function of the state in this connexion is the establishment and the enforcement of law. He does not deny the necessity for other forms of state action in the spheres which have been already discussed. But so far as the general organization of production is concerned, his essential conception of the role of the state is the conception of the law-giver. For the authoritarian, on the other hand, the characteristic function of the state is, not the law, but the quantitative plan. Indeed, since he invests the state with the responsibility for the specific acts of production, for him the law is a nuisance, its fixity and its generality inappropriate; since the situation to be dealt with changes from moment to moment and from place to place, any attempt to prescribe in advance the form of state action is a hampering limitation. The contrast must not be pressed too far; the authoritarian submits to some laws, the Classical liberal conceives of some public discretion.

---

[1] On all this, see the admirable formulations of the late Henry Simons in the various papers reprinted in *Economic Policy for a Free Society*, especially p. 160.

But, in the main, it holds : the System of Economic Freedom, so far as the organization of production was concerned, was a system of rules which was supposed to make individual freedom conducive to social advantage.

(vii) *The Classical Economists and the Forms of Government*

There is still one question left for us to answer in this attempt to establish perspective : what was the attitude of the Classical Economists to the ultimate problem of the forms of government ? The state is distinguished from all other organs of social co-operation by the fact that, even in pure logical constructions, it must be endowed with an irreducible minimum of coercive authority. However individualistic our norms in regard to other social institutions, we cannot divest the state itself of some power of ultimate coercion without risking the disintegration of all the rest. Assumptions regarding the constitution of such authority must, therefore, be an implicit feature of any theory of policy which aspires to be general in scope.

Now this is not a matter on which we should expect to find any strong uniformity of opinion among the group of men whose attitude we are examining. The different leading members lived at different times in a rapidly changing history : and, although some of them may have thought otherwise, it is not true that either the utilitarian or the individualist postulates necessarily dictate a unique solution of the problem of the appropriate form of government — especially if that problem is considered with some regard to conditions of time and space. The most that we could expect to find would be certain movements and divergences of opinion which

had some continuing relation to the other elements in
the theory of policy, relations, perhaps, as it were, of
partial rather than total derivatives.

Such relations are, I believe, very clearly discernible
and it is not an inappropriate conclusion to this survey
to consider them, however briefly.

At the beginning of our period we have Smith and
Hume. I am not aware of any utterance of Smith which
would indicate a preference above all others for one
form of government, although there are many indicating
distastes and antipathies. But Hume, as usual, had a
considered position which was one of decided conservatism in the ultimate philosophical sense. It is true
that as an exercise, as it were, he worked out an idea of a
perfect commonwealth which differed in some substantial
respects from the one in which he happened to live. But
his main judgment was quite definitely that the onus of
demonstration lay with the advocates of change in the
status quo. " It is not with forms of government, as
with other artificial contrivances ; where an old engine
may be rejected, if we can discover another more
accurate and commodious, or where trials may safely be
made, even though the success be doubtful. An established government has an infinite advantage, by that
very circumstance of its being established ; the bulk of
mankind being governed by authority, not reason, and
never attributing authority to anything that has not the
recommendation of antiquity. To temper, therefore, in
this affair, or try experiments merely upon the credit of a
supposed argument and philosophy, can never be the
part of a wise magistrate, who will bear a reverence to
what carries the marks of age : and though he may
attempt some improvements for the public good, yet
he will adjust his innovations, as much as possible, to
the ancient fabric, and preserve entire the chief pillars

and supports of the constitution." [1]

This is perhaps the best statement extant of the broad basis of utilitarian conservatism. No Divine Rights are invoked, no mystical general will postulated. There is no appeal to an implicit justice in History with a capital H, no suggestion of some latent best self in each which it is the duty of the best people (neo-Hegelians) to see elicited. The sole justification of any social order is utility ; but, since the social impulses are intermittent and fragile, the presumption is usually in favour of enduring the evils we know, rather than flying to others that we know not of. Existing constitutions are "botched and inaccurate", but only "gentle alterations" are likely to bring a balance of good over bad. Antiquity is not good in itself. But if regard for antiquity is conducive to good citizenship, what folly not to make use of it.

The attitude of Jeremy Bentham in his earlier years was not the same as this. The youthful Bentham was much too zealous a law reformer to set any store by regard for established institutions. The "Matchless Constitution" of Blackstone (not of Hume, who, of

---

[1] Hume, *Essays, Moral, Political and Literary* (edited Green and Grose), vol. i, p. 480. It should be noted that this almost Burkean attitude did not lead Hume, as it did Burke, into the extreme position of decrying the usefulness of any speculation on the best form of government. " As one form of government must be allowed more perfect than another, independent of the manners and humours of particular men : why may we not inquire what is the most perfect of all, though the common botched and inaccurate governments seem to serve the purposes of society, and though it be not so easy to establish a new system of government, as to build a vessel upon a new construction. The subject is surely the most worthy curiosity of any the wit of man can possibly devise. And who knows, if this controversy were fixed by the universal consent of the wise and learned, but, in some future age, an opportunity might be afforded of reducing the theory to practice, either by the dissolution of some old government, or by the combination of men to form a new one, in some distant part of the world. In all cases, it must be advantageous to know what is most perfect in the kind, that we may be able to bring any real constitution or form of government as near it as possible, by such gentle alterations as may not give too great disturbance to society."

course, never thought it matchless) was the subject of
unending ironies. But there was no strong disposition
to political reform as such. The shrill declamations of
revolutionaries disgusted Bentham no less than the
pompous mumbo-jumbo of the mystical reactionaries.
Provided that he could secure reform of the law and
what he conceived to be proper administrative policies,
he was comparatively indifferent to the actual constitution of the sovereign power. He was just as willing to
furnish codes for the Empress of Russia as for the
French National Assembly.

As is well known, this attitude did not persist. Hope
deferred maketh the heart sick : the many disappoint-
ments and frustrations of Bentham's middle years,
especially the fiasco of the *Panopticon*, led him to re-
consider the theory of the forms of government in the
light of his general principles. This led him to the conclusion that, unless the making of laws and their
administration were not in some sense within the control
of those who were affected by them, there were likely to
develop clashes of interest. Since direct democracy was
impracticable outside the confines of the village or the
city state, this led in turn to the demand for government on a basis of democratic representation. The most
famous statement of this point of view, which was the
political rallying-ground of the early utilitarians (in the
narrow sense of the word) and the philosophical radicals,
is, of course, to be found in James Mill's famous essay on
" Government " in the supplement to the fifth edition
of the *Encyclopaedia Britannica*.[1] But the essentials are
all to be found (without the lapses regarding the position
of women which so grieved John Stuart Mill) in Bentham's
Plan of Parliamentary Reform in the form of a Catechism.[2]

[1] See Sir Ernest Barker's reprint, Cambridge University Press, 1937.
[2] Bentham, *op. cit.* vol. iii, pp. 433-577.

The same sentiments were also expressed, albeit with somewhat greater caution as regards immediate action, by Ricardo in his *Observations on Parliamentary Reform*.[1]

Thus, by the end of the first quarter of the nineteenth century, the strict application of utilitarian theory had given rise to a general *rationale* of universal suffrage. James Mill might exclude women on the ground that they were adequately represented by their husbands. He might in practice be content with the extension of the franchise to the lower middle-class voter. The theory of the subject, however, as propounded by this group, logically involved complete democracy.

But this view was not generally accepted, even among those who were certainly to be counted as progressives according to the standards of the day. The Classical Economists of the day were supporters of the Reform Bill. But they were not all supporters of universal suffrage. There was a division among reformers in this respect. Bentham and Ricardo had argued that

---

[1] Ricardo, *Works* (edited McCulloch), pp. 551-556. It is worth observing that McCulloch's introduction on the Life and Writing of Ricardo essentially misrepresents Ricardo in this respect. According to McCulloch, Ricardo " did not . . . agree with the radical reformers in their plan of universal suffrage ; he thought the elective franchise should be given to all who possessed a certain amount of property ; but he was of opinion, that while it would be a very hazardous experiment, no practical good would result from giving the franchise indiscriminately to all " (*ibid.* p. xxxi). But this is not the attitude of the *Observations*. Ricardo indeed deprecates the talk of universal suffrage, declares himself in favour of caution and states that " an extension of the suffrage, far short of making it universal, will substantially secure to the people the good government they wish for ". But he attacks the position of those who oppose universal suffrage on the ground that it would result in infringements of the rights of property, and, in the same sentence as the one quoted above in which he urges a limited extension first, he goes on to say, " I feel confident that the effects of the measure which would satisfy me would have so beneficial an effect on the public mind — would be the means of so rapidly increasing the knowledge and intelligence of the public, that, in a limited space of time after this first measure of reform were granted, we might, with the utmost safety, extend the right of voting for Members of Parliament to every class of the people ". An extremely amiable picture of Ricardo as an advocate of Parliamentary Reform s given by his friendly expostulations to Trower, who was of a different political persuasion. *Letters of Ricardo to Trower* (edited Bonar and Hollander), pp. 60-71.

there was no danger to property, no menace of levelling tendencies implicit in such a system. But this was not the view of the Whig as distinct from the Radical reformers. Macaulay, who is not to be counted a Classical Economist, but who was an archetypal Whig reformer in this respect, devoted one of the most forceful passages in his review of James Mill on Government to precisely this question. "How is it possible", he asks, "for any person who holds the doctrines of Mr. Mill to doubt that the rich, in a democracy, such as that which he recommends, would be pillaged as unmercifully as under a Turkish Pacha?"; and then, after arguing that, on Mill's own principles, it is in the short-run interest of the very poor to despoil property: "The civilized part of the world has now nothing to fear from the hostility of savage nations. Once the deluge of barbarism has passed over it, to destroy and to fertilize : and in the present state of mankind we enjoy a full security against that calamity. That flood will no more return to cover the earth. But is it possible that in the bosom of civilization itself may be engendered the malady which shall destroy it ? Is it possible that institutions shall be established which, without the help of earthquake, of famine, of pestilence, or of the foreign sword, may undo the work of so many ages of wisdom and glory, and gradually sweep away taste, literature, science, commerce, manufactures, everything but the rude arts necessary to the support of animal life ? Is it possible that in two or three hundred years, a few lean and half-naked fishermen may divide with owls and foxes the ruins of the greatest European cities — may wash their nets against the relics of her gigantic docks and build their huts out of the capitals of her stately cathedrals ? If the principles of Mr. Mill be sound, we say without hesitation, that the form of government which he recommends will assuredly produce all this. But if these principles be unsound, if the reasonings which we have opposed to them be just, the higher and middling orders are the natural representatives of the human race. Their interest may be opposed in some things to that of their poorer contemporaries ; but it is identical with that of the innumerable generations which are to follow." [1]

This view, which was probably the majority view of mid-nineteenth-century liberals, was certainly held by Senior. In his journal kept in France in 1849 there is an account of a conversation with Beaumont which states this quite unequivocally. "Much reflection and the power of following and retaining a long train of reasoning are necessary to enable men thoroughly to master the premisses which prove that, though it is in the power of human institutions to make everybody poor, they cannot make everybody rich ; that they can diffuse misery, but not happiness. Among philosophers this is a conviction ; among the higher and middle classes — that is to say, among those to whom an equal distribution of wealth would be obviously unfavourable — this is a prejudice founded partly on the authority of those to whom they look up, and partly on their own apparent interest. But the apparent interest of the lower classes is the other way. They grossly miscalculate the number and value of the prizes in the lottery of life, they think that they have drawn little better than blanks, and believe those who tell them that if all the high lots were abolished everybody might have a hundred-pound prize.

"As long as this is the political economy of the poor, there seem to be only three means of governing a densely peopled country in which they form the large majority.

[1] Macaulay, *Speeches on Politics and Literature* (Everyman edition), pp. 428-430.

One is to exclude them from political life. This is our English policy, and where we have deviated from it, as has been done in some boroughs, the sort of constituents that the freemen make show what would be our fate under universal suffrage. Another is the existence among them of a blind devotion to the laws and customs of the country. The small cantons of Switzerland, Uri, Schwyz, Unterwalden, Glarus, Zug, Appenzell, and the Grisons are pure democracies. The males of legal age form the sovereign power, without even the intervention of representatives. But they venerate their clergy, their men of birth and of wealth, and their institutions, and form practically the aristocratic portion of Switzerland. A third plan is to rely on military power — to arm and discipline the higher and middle classes, and support them by a regular army trained to implicit obedience." [1]

The frame of mind, it will be observed, bears a strong family resemblance to the frame of mind in which Walter Bagehot, more than twenty years later, confessed, " As a theoretical writer I can venture to say, what no elected Member of Parliament, Conservative or Liberal, can venture to say, that I am exceedingly afraid of the ignorant multitude of the new constituencies ".[2] It is clear that, in the ranks of the reformers, two views concerning the forms of government had developed. The one, the radical wing, wished to push forward to what Bentham called " virtually universal suffrage " and rejected the argument that this would be inimical to the general framework of economic activity which they thought desirable. The other, the Whig or middle Liberal wing, thought this view to be mistaken and took their stand on the property qualification.

---

[1] Senior, *Journals Kept in France and Italy*, vol. i, pp. 150-152.
[2] Bagehot, *The English Constitution*, Introduction to the 2nd edition (World's Classics edition), p. 276.

Where did John Stuart Mill stand in relation to this issue ? As so often, his position was very individual and very significant.

It is well known that to the end of his life Mill remained true to the radicalism of his early youth, in that he gave full and vigorous support to the extension of the franchise in this country. It was one of the main contentions, moreover, of his work on *Representative Government* that what he called the ideally best polity was one embodying some version of the representative principle with a basis in universal suffrage, including the enfranchisement of women. Much more explicitly historical in outlook than his predecessors, he was willing to make all kinds of concessions to the limitations of time and place. A case was to be made out for despotism in certain circumstances : even slavery had some justification at certain periods ; the institution of monarchical government had performed useful and, indeed, essential functions in the past. He was prepared to countenance a literary test — the ability to read and write and perform a simple calculation in the rule of three.[1] He urged strongly that the receipt of public relief should be a disqualification from voting, and he wished direct taxation to be extended to almost the lowest income receivers in order that they might have a due sense of responsibility in voting upon issues involving the spending of public money.[2] But no one has ever stated more forcibly than Mill did the case against the exclusion of any class from the right of voting, provided that the general tests of readiness for representative government in general were satisfied. " Does Parliament, or almost any of the members composing it, even for an instant look at any question with the eyes of a working man ?

[1] J. S. Mill, *Considerations on Representative Government* (Blackwell reprint), p. 213.   [2] *Ibid.* p. 215.

When a subject arises in which the labourers as such have an interest, is it regarded from any point of view but that of the employers of labour ?   I do not say that the working men's view of these questions is in general nearer the truth than the other : but it is sometimes quite as near ; and in any case it ought to be respectfully listened to, instead of being, as it is, not merely turned away from, but ignored." [1]   He was no less eloquent in support of the claims of women. [2]

Nevertheless, he was not happy at the prospect of unmitigated democracy, as hitherto conceived.   He thought it to be liable to two great infirmities : the suppression of minorities by the majority and the failure to produce an adequate supply of first-rate governmental talent and to foster the preponderance of intelligence in the general conduct of public business.   He felt passionately about these matters.   The essay *On Liberty* is one long protest against the tendency in contemporary societies to crush individual variations.   The *Considerations on Representative Government* must be regarded as being as much a plea for adequate safeguards against the abuses of democracy as an argument for proceeding towards its realization.   Certainly, to the modern reader, the novelty of the work consists far more in the sections

[1] *Ibid.* p. 143.   Mill continues, " On the question of strikes, for instance, it is doubtful if there is so much as one among the leading members of either House who is not firmly convinced that the reason of the matter is unqualifiedly on the side of the masters, and that the men's view of it is simply absurd.   Those who have studied the question know well how far this is from being the case ; and in how different, and how infinitely less superficial a manner the point would have to be argued, if the classes who strike were able to make themselves heard in Parliament."

[2] *Ibid.* p. 222 *seq.*   " In the preceding argument ", he says, ". . . I have taken no account of difference of sex.   I consider it to be as entirely irrelevant to political rights as difference in height or in the colour of the hair.   All human beings have the same interest in good government ; the welfare of all is alike affected by it, and they have equal need of a voice in it to secure their share of its benefits.   If there be any difference, women require it more than men, since, being physically weaker, they are more dependent on law and society for protection."

proposing remedies for abuses, than in the sections urging
democracy as such, magnificently argued as these are.
For the democratic argument was not new. What was
new was the recognition on the part of a radical, such
as Mill, that democracy as such was not enough.

In recognizing the dangers, of course, Mill was not
altogether out of harmony with men such as Macaulay
and Senior : there is a passage in *Representative Government* which expresses much the same apprehensions as
the passages which I have quoted from these authors.[1]
But whereas they were led by these apprehensions to
rely upon a property qualification for voting, Mill
rejected this unless as a temporary makeshift, and
relied rather upon two novel expedients : a scheme for
proportional representation, almost the first of its kind,
put forward by a Mr. Hare, which he thought would give
effective representation to minorities and facilitate the
choice of national figures as candidates ; and plural
voting based, not on property, but upon function and
education : bankers, merchants, manufacturers, members

---

[1] Mill, *op. cit.* pp. 182-183. " In all countries there is a majority of poor, a
minority who, in contradistinction, may be called rich. Between these two
classes, on many questions, there is complete opposition of apparent interest.
We will suppose the majority sufficiently intelligent to be aware that it is not
for their advantage to weaken the security of property, and that it would be
weakened by any act of arbitrary spoliation. But is there not a considerable
danger lest they should throw upon the possessors of what is called realized
property, and upon the larger incomes, an unfair share, or even the whole, of
the burden of taxation ; and having done so, add to the amount without scruple,
expending the proceeds in modes supposed to conduce to the profit and advantage
of the labouring class ? Suppose, again, a minority of skilled labourers, a
majority of unskilled : the experience of many trade unions, unless they are
greatly calumniated, justifies the apprehension that equality of earnings might
be imposed as an obligation, and that piecework, payment by the hour, and all
practices which enable superior industry or abilities to gain a superior reward
might be put down. Legislative attempts to raise wages, limitation of competition in the labour market, taxes or restrictions on machinery, and on
improvements of all kinds tending to dispense with any of the existing labour —
even, perhaps, protection of the home producer against foreign industry — are
very natural (I do not venture to say whether probable) results of a feeling of
class interest in a governing majority of manual labourers."

of the liberal professions, university graduates, might, he thought, be allowed more than one vote. The details of this latter proposal were left vague. But he was emphatic that " in this direction lies the true ideal of representative government ; and that to work towards it, by the best practical contrivances which can be found is the path of real political improvement ".[1]

Thus, by the end of our period, the impulse to pure democracy, which had shown itself so strongly in some of the writers of the middle years, had begun, not perhaps to recoil, but at least to develop doubts and to suggest new devices, not reconcilable with the old ideas of pure democracy, save by appeal to some overriding general conception supposed to embody the best ideals of the democratic spirit. Mill had an heroic belief in the powers of reason and persuasion ; and he was not one to turn back on a course which seemed to him to be generally right. But I do not think that anyone reading the works of the later part of Mill's life can fail to be unaware of an underlying anxiety, a scarcely suppressed fear : [2] will the democratic society of the future have restraint enough to preserve the sacred liberty of the human spirit, and wisdom and self-control enough to ensure its own progress and stability ? — a momentous question to which, as yet, time has not given a convincing answer.

(viii) *Conclusion*

I should like to end these lectures, as I began them, by emphasizing their purely historical and descriptive intention.

[1] *Ibid.* p. 218.
[2] Cf. the Introduction to the posthumous *Chapters on Socialism, op. cit.* pp. 217-223.

The field they have covered embraces some of the most difficult, some of the most active, issues still confronting human society. How interesting it would be, having surveyed the Classical contribution to the solution of these problems, to proceed to examine to what extent, according to our lights and our ethical postulates, these contributions are in any sense valid. To what extent is their theory of the market sustained by the results of more recent analysis? How far were they justified in the hope that financial controls (about the exact nature of which they never reached agreement) were sufficient to maintain the stability of the envelope of aggregate demand which the System of Economic Freedom postulated? Did their theory of property overlook overriding technical influences tending to general monopoly? In what measure has this theory been rendered obsolete by the development of joint stock companies and the limited liability principle? How do our present views regarding population tendencies affect our conception of the limits of the eleemosynary function? Were the Classical Economists right in their apprehensions of over-all collectivism?

These are all serious problems which well deserve our best efforts at contemporary solution. But they have not been the problems to which I have been directing your attention in these lectures. All that I have done is to try to explain to you, in the broadest possible outline, what the English Classical Economists held to be the appropriate principles of economic policy and, again in the broadest possible outline, the reasons which underlay these beliefs.

If, in the course of so doing, I have led you, despite their detractors, to have some regard for their candour and their public spirit, I should not regard that as incompatible with the limits which I have striven to observe. For whatever we may think of their theories on purely intellectual grounds, I am sure that, in that respect at least, we should find something in their work which is both admirable and inspiring.

SELECT BIBLIOGRAPHY

THE original sources of all quotations used in these lectures are given in the footnotes. The following is a short list of commentaries and critical histories which have some general bearing on the topics under discussion.

BOWLEY, M. *Nassau Senior and Classical Economics*, London, 1937.

CANNAN, E. *A Review of Economic Theory*, London, 1929.

DICEY, A. V. *Law and Public Opinion in England during the Nineteenth Century*, 2nd Edition, London, 1914.

HALÉVY, E. *The Growth of Philosophical Radicalism*, Cheap Edition, London, 1934.

HAYEK, F. *Individualism and Economic Order*, London, 1948.

HUTT, W. H. *Economists and the Public*, London, 1936.

MACGREGOR, D. H. *Economic Thought and Policy*, London, 1949.

SCHATZ, A. *L'Individualisme, économique et social*, Paris, 1907.

SCHÜLLER, R. *Die klassische Nationalökonomie und ihre Gegner*, Berlin, 1895.

STEPHEN, L. *History of English Thought in the Eighteenth Century*, 3rd Edition, London, 1902.

The English Utilitarians, London, 1900.

TAUSSIG, F. *Wages and Capital: an Examination of the Wages Fund Doctrine*, New York, 1897.

VINER, J. " Adam Smith and Laissez-Faire ", being Chapter V of *Adam Smith, 1776-1926: Lectures to Commemorate the Sesquicentennial of the Publication of the " Wealth of Nations "*, by J. M. Clark & Others, Chicago, 1928.

" Bentham and J. S. Mill: the Utilitarian Background ", *American Economic Review*, March 1949.

INDEX OF PROPER NAMES

Smith, Vera : 32
Spencer, Herbert : his conception of the functions of the state, 36 ; his individualism based on the theory of natural rights and antithetical to utilitarianism, 48, 49

Taussig, W. : on the use of the wage fund theory by the Classical Economists, 110 n.
Thiebault : his account of the alleged conversation between Mercier de la Rivière and Catherine the Great, cited, 35
Tocqueville, Alexis de : quoted by Senior on the *droit au travail*, 138-139
Tooke, T. : his dispute with Overstone a disproof of the alleged unanimity of the Classical School, 3 ; cited as representative of Banking School, 32 ; on limited liability, 55 n.
Torrens, R. : a Classical Economist, 2 ; his development of the theory of comparative advantage, 16 ; cited as representative of Currency School, 31 ; repudiation of *laissez-faire*, 44 n. ; urges formation of compensation fund for relief of displaced operatives, 104

Viner, Jacob: on Adam Smith's alleged *Harmonielehre*, 25 n. ; on Bentham on the functions of the state, 39, 40 ; on Halévy's misunderstanding of the Classical Economists, 191

Wallas, Graham : his *Life of Francis Place* cited, 73 n. ; cited on Place's attitude to the future of trade unions, 108 n.
Webb, S. and B. : cited on the attitude of Senior to trade unions, 108 n.
Wheatley, John: his second thoughts on currency, 31 ; use of term *laissez-faire*, 44 n.

THE END